Be Still My Soul

"A Calling from Beyond the Veil"

Helen R. Biddulph-Bertler

Guidon
Provo, UT

The Guidon colophon is the trademark of the Biddulph Family Creations of Provo, Utah. The Biddulph family name derives from its earlier name *Guidon*, meaning a guide or standard bearer. Tradition holds that members of the *Guidon* family occupied Britain with William the Conqueror, and settled in central Britain at a township known as Biddulph, near Staffordshire, England, at which time they assumed the name of Biddulph.

Copyright 2014: by Helen R. Biddulph-Bertler

ISBN-10: 1495937194
ISBN-13: 978-1495937194

Dedicated to my "beloved" David, husband; Rolf, children; Chris, Anna, Laura, and Mohna and their spouses, David's father; Don, David's girlfriend; Kristen, and David's grandparents; Howard and Colleen Biddulph, and many other extended family and friends.

"And charity suffereth long, and is kind and envieth not, and is not puffed up, seeketh not her own, is not easily provoked, thinketh no evil, and rejoiceth not in iniquity but rejoiceth in the truth, beareth all things, believeth all things, hopeth all things, endureth all things...if you have not charity, ye are nothing, for charity never faileth...but charity is the pure love of christ, and it endureth forever; and whoso is found possessed of it at the last day, it shall be well with him."
(Moroni 7:45-47)

Table of Contents

PREFACE vii

ACKNOWLEDGEMENTS ix

INTRODUCTION 1

CHAPTER ONE: The Diagnosis 3

CHAPTER TWO: David's Dream 11

CHAPTER THREE: Ups and Downs 25

CHAPTER FOUR: As I Have Loved You 31

CHAPTER FIVE: Trusting In the Lord 37

CHAPTER SIX: Mighty Miracles 41

CHAPTER SEVEN: Be Still My Soul 51

CHAPTER EIGHT: David, Our Beloved 57

CHAPTER NINE: Angels among Us 63

CHAPTER TEN: David's Eulogy 71

CHAPTER ELEVEN: Let Not Your Heart Be Troubled 89

CHAPTER TWELVE: Ministering of Angels 101

CHAPTER THIRTEEN: Family Testimonies 127

NOTES 149

WORKS CITED 153

PREFACE

"Be Still My Soul" was inspired through much prayer, study and reflection. This true story is based upon my personal thoughts and experiences watching my son suffer and pass away due to an incurable form of cancer. It was the most painful, yet most spiritual, experience I have ever encountered in my lifetime. We can learn much through our tribulations, especially the heartache that comes through the death of a loved one. Wayne Shute, an Emeritus professor of BYU, and author of a number of professional books, provides advice along this topic in his most helpful book, The Death of a Loved One: Life's Most Severe test. He claims, "As in life, there is much to learn, so likewise in death. Life after the death of a loved one can turn out to be one of the most productive periods of learning in our entire lives."[1] I hope to encourage all who read to exert more faith, hope and charity into their daily lives and more fully internalize what is of most importance in this lifetime.

I've studied the scriptures and the following books to support my claims: Angels, Agents of Light, Love, And Power" by Donald W. Parry, What's On the Other Side, by Brent L. Top, The Message by Lance Richardson, The Life Beyond by Richard Millet and Joseph McConkie, Life Everlasting" by Duane S. Crowther, The Death of a Loved One: Life's Most Severe Test," by R. Wayne Shute and

Teachings of the Presidents of the Church by the Church of Jesus Christ of latter-Day Saints.

The words to the following hymns: "Abide with Me Tis Eventide" and "Be Still My Soul" have been included in this book. I've also included scriptural passages at the beginning of each chapter. Many pictures have been added to bring to life these actual events. Through my son's loving character, I've tried to portray the true characteristics of charity; the greatest attribute we could ever possess in this lifetime! I pray the hearts of those reading will be touched, and if necessary, softened. I speak with much frankness, yet sincerity, and write this out of love for my Heavenly Father and Savior Jesus Christ, my family on this earth and above, and for the benefit of my fellowmen.

ACKNOWLEDGEMENTS

I want to pay special tribute to all our children and their spouses, including David's sweetheart Kristen, my siblings, grandchildren, and parents, who have stood by my side in ways that cannot be completely counted or expressed, even though I attempt to do so through the writing of this book.

I am incredibly thankful for my husband Rolf, who was most supportive and dedicated in nursing, filling and buying prescriptions, babysitting, purchasing treats, chauffeuring, and running errands. His undaunting support was there for us constantly during this difficult time. Words cannot express my love and gratitude for such a man in my life! A special thanks to our dear friends, especially the Easterbrooks, Osmonds, Hughes, McCues, as well as Candy Burton. Through your willingness to serve, I was able to write such a beautiful story! Thank you, Leanne Hughes, Ute Patterson, Diane Shapcott, Sandy Stevenson, Eva Herrey, Debby Rittel, and Laura MacDonald for your undying friendship.

I am thankful to all who contributed testimonies and/or suggestions to the manuscript: Howard Biddulph, Colleen Biddulph, Laura Alms, Chris Gow, Don Gow, Rolf Bertler, Mohna Thuernagle, Kristen Bean, and Barbara Sorensen, who also contributed to the editing of this book. Special thanks to Catherine Vail, Mohna Thuernagle and my husband, Rolf for your precious photography!

INTRODUCTION

On the early morning of July 28, 2013, my nineteen year old son, David, courageously passed away after battling an aggressive, inoperable form of cancer which attacks the blood vessels. Angiosarcoma is extremely rare; only between twenty to sixty people, usually children, and sometimes teenagers, are inflicted with this type of cancer per year in the United States. The cancer had eaten away most of his left hip, metastasized into his neck, which was bulging by the time of his passing, and finally into his lungs, which collapsed during the last few days of his life. In the end, it became necessary to sedate him because he would greatly panic due to extreme shortness of breath, even with a full breathing mask. An intrathecal pump had been inserted through his spinal cord to inject a more efficient flow of pain medication, basically working to freeze his extremities.

The pump had become necessary because his past injections and medications were not providing enough relief anymore due to toxicity. He found only occasional relief over the span of a year of time. For the last two weeks of his life, Rolf and I, and sometimes other family members, slept in hospital beds close by his side because we could not find peace anywhere else. I can bear testimony to the fact though that God will not leave us comfortless, especially when we are obedient and accepting of his will on our behalf. There have not been adequate words to express my feelings, but I did receive some understanding of how "Mother Mary" might have felt.

We prayed fervently for the pump to work, and it finally did after two days of sheer agony on his part, and then my final words of desperation to Heavenly Father when he struggled to breathe at the end, "Please Lord, take him soon, this is too much for us all to bear!" We prayed earnestly on many other occasions as I held him closely when he cried out in extreme agony. The Lord took him within hours after my last prayer for his release while he was still in mortality.

Would I ever have imagined I would pray for the Lord to take my beloved son? David's patience, courage, and unconditional love were truly evident throughout his lifetime, but his endurance was greatly tested through this most painful ordeal. He has won the battle victoriously, and the angels surely rejoiced and brought him home!

CHAPTER ONE: The Diagnosis

"Father if thou be willing remove this cup from me, nevertheless not my will, but thine be done."1

Just a little more than a year before David's passing, we had visited him in Branson, Missouri for a few days of fun together. He was living with his sister Laura and her family in Mt. Vernon at the time. We discussed some of the problems and challenges he was personally facing. We also were having problems and misunderstandings within the family that were causing much pain and division. He listened and understood where we were coming from. He was always good at showing empathy with most everyone he came in contact with. Little did we know he already had angiosarcoma!

Angiosarcoma is an especially cruel cancer and there are no warning signs. Once you feel the pain of this disease, it is already too late, especially if it has metastasized. David started feeling pain in his left hip within a month after we parted that summer of 2012. At first, he experienced a painful burning surge down his leg, which grew into a very extreme form of sciatica. He often compared his leg pain to the intensity of electrocution. David tried so many things, including massage and special exercises to no avail. He went to see many doctors, and even went to the emergency room on many occasions, just to return back home with no relief. He decided to fly back to live with his father in Vanderhoof, B.C

Canada in November of that same year.

David was told repeatedly by various nurses, each time he visited the emergency room, that nothing could be done and was reassured his pain was most likely in his head. He came to the conclusion that these nurses probably thought he was lying about his pain so he could get drugs! I was absolutely livid when I heard of these experiences because he did not get much relief from his excruciating pain and couldn't sleep or eat for months. He finally did receive x-rays, but nothing was found at first. He painfully managed to come from Vanderhoof to Vancouver Island with his father, so I could see him the day after Christmas of 2012.

By the time I saw him by the end of December, he looked like a holocaust victim weighing in around 108 lbs; I was completely horrified! He cried out in agonizing pain constantly until his father took him to a nearby hospital in Nanaimo, B.C, where they took our concerns more seriously. He was given Ketorolac, an anti inflammatory drug, which gave him some temporary relief for his unbelievable pain. I was teaching middle school in Pleasant Grove Utah at the time and was expected back to continue teaching, so I had to leave for a time. Soon after returning home, I received a call from him. He told me he had been admitted into the Nanaimo hospital for tests. I was relieved that someone was finally taking him seriously.

Earlier, David had been told his pain was most likely a

CHAPTER ONE: The Diagnosis

"referred pain," from a slipped disc in his back. Unfortunately, the x-rays given by those who disbelieved in him were taken of his back, but the real problem was not located there, so of course those x-rays showed nothing. One day, as a massage therapist came to give David a "rub down," he screamed hysterically when the therapist tried to rub his hip. This actually was a blessing, for it showed us where the true problem was really located. Further testing revealed his left hip to be completely deteriorated by some form of lesion or tumor.

It was very hard to fathom that my supposedly healthy son could have such a condition. I do remember feeling somewhat peaceful though, thinking this to mean the tumor was benign, or if cancerous, at least treatable. David never sought revenge by writing a nasty letter to those who had misdiagnosed and disbelieved in him for so many months, causing him additional pain and suffering. It had been suggested he write such a letter, but he never did. David was not one to cause disharmony or speak harshly of anyone.

We imagined it to be just a matter of time before experiencing the success of his hip replacement surgery. He even was put in the wing of the Vancouver hospital for this type of surgery. We now had to wait, which seemed like an eternity, for the results of his biopsy. I shall never forget the day we got the heart-wrenching prognosis. I was in the middle of a faculty meeting when my husband Rolf came in to tell me privately of David's condition. Rolf is not one to "beat around the bush!" He always got straight to the point, believing it did no good to put icing on something that could not be palatable.

He looked me square in the eyes and sadly stated, "David is being called back home to Heavenly Father!" The sting of his words struck me with such wrenching force that I couldn't breathe for a moment. I then cried, "Don't tell me this, don't tell me this, how do you know for sure?" Rolf then calmly told me that David had been the one to tell him that he had been given six months to two years to live. The lesions that were pressing upon his sciatic nerve had been found to be cancerous tumors that had already metastasized and were inoperable due to their location in his blood vessels. He then added the worst news of all; his cancer was at stage four, and there was no known cure. This was the beginning of my grieving process.

I asked my father for a priesthood blessing for comfort and understanding. In this most important blessing, I was told David still had a short mission here in mortality, but the Lord had a very special mission waiting for him on the other side of the veil. I felt that it meant in the near future, and could not get myself to argue with the Lord. I came to accept this through much prayer, study, and contemplation. In the classic bestseller, <u>Life Everlasting,</u> much has been said about our responsibilities beyond the veil, "There is ample evidence, from both the teachings of Latter-day Saint General Authorities

CHAPTER ONE: The Diagnosis

and from the statements made by those who have returned to earth from beyond the veil that many die to fulfill responsibilities in the spirit world."2 These readings have brought much peace and understanding, and the promptings I've received through the Holy Ghost, have helped me realize what steps to gradually take along this painful journey. I knew it to be my responsibility to help prepare my son for complete acceptance of the Lord's will for him.

After learning of his prognosis, we immediately flew to Vancouver to be with David thinking he must be devastated. To our surprise, David was calm and happy. It helped me tremendously to see how accepting David was of his situation, but I could see right away that he had not realized the Lord's will just yet. He hoped he might have years to live and wanted to fight the disease. He seemed unafraid, which amazed me. Then again, he always amazed me! We could only stay for ten days on this first particular visit because I was still teaching at the time. David began radiation treatment while we were still in Vancouver on this particular visit.

I felt uplifted due to his calmness and acceptance of his circumstances. I thought I had come to uplift him, but in reality, found him to be the real gift giver. Just before I had to leave to return back to Utah, I caught him conversing on the phone with a friend providing guidance with a problem. I was astounded at his strength, especially after just receiving his own devastating news, but David never was devastated. He always tried to make the most out of every obstacle he faced, and there were many.

Radiation therapy can be deceiving, at first it gave David much relief, which mistakenly gave him the perception he was improving. It was discovered that his tumor was eight centimeters wide; about the size of a large orange! We also learned there were already microscopic cancerous nodes on his lungs. At this time in January, I remember him mentioning his neck was somewhat sore, but thought it was from lying in bed so much. He sweat profusely, but was happy the nurses were able to cut back on his doses of Hydromorphone and Ketorolac in regard to these first treatments. He was using crutches by this time because most of his left hip had been eaten away by this vicious tumor.

Our first visit was very sweet; I recall him looking so angelic. Most of the children were able to meet with us in Vancouver to support David after learning of his diagnosis. David wanted to fight the disease, not only with radiation, but also with chemotherapy treatments. Unfortunately, it wasn't long before the side effects of these treatments revealed their true, ugly faces. It was almost an insurmountable task for me to leave and go back to Utah. Upon returning home, David soon began mentioning bad side effects. However, it wasn't until I saw, that I fully understood. He had downplayed his whole condition because he wanted to be positive thinking and not have others worried. I respected this, so I kept my public

CHAPTER ONE: The Diagnosis

comments as positive as I could, especially on Face book.

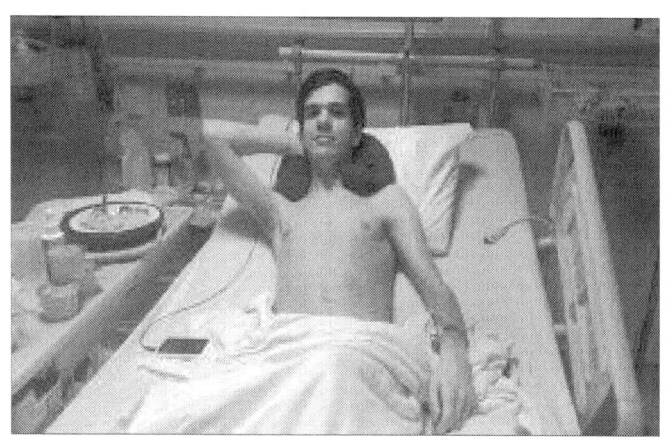

(David in the Vancouver General Hospital for first radiations)

(Laura Alms, Chris and Laura Gow, Don Gow, Anna Chow, Helen Bertler, Rolf Bertler, and twins, Isabelle and Abigail Gow on first visit with David)

CHAPTER TWO: David's Dream

"When you are in the service of your fellow beings, ye are only in the service of your God"1

It was difficult being apart from my son in February, especially when I went back to teach again, I really had trouble concentrating. My students and administration understood when I decided to resign, a decision I shall forever be grateful I chose. It brought peace to be able to devote all my energy to David and my other children who were suffering emotionally. I knew I was to return back to Canada once March rolled forth. My intuition told me that David did not have a lot of time left, though I kept this mainly to myself at first to not upset anyone. I was very grateful that the new service missionaries from the Church of Jesus Christ of Latter-day Saints with the last name of "Easterbrook" were devoting much time to David, especially while I was gone in February. They were "heaven sent" and were there to visit, provide treats, and uplift my son; an awesome blessing from Heavenly Father.

I did share the information that David had a short time left in mortality with a few important people; Debbie Osmond was one of them. I had come to know her through working closely in our church ward on Sundays. She led and I played the piano for the children's music time most Sundays. I felt impressed to ask her if Donny could possibly help set up a special dream for David, that of meeting Celine Dion. Celine had been David's inspiration since he was four years old and Donny knew her personally! This was no easy task, even for Donny, but I kept praying for this dream to be realized.

In the meantime, I focused on quitting my teaching job and welcomed a letter of recommendation before leaving for a long span of time to Canada. A parent of one of my students, Candy Burton, set up a fund raiser for David's dream to come true. She wanted to fly David to Las Vegas with hotel and tickets included. It was looking like David's dream, at least of going to see her perform, was going to come true. I was relieved that David couldn't wait to go on this trip, knowing there was not much time left, and he wasn't even close to the point of accepting this just yet.

When we finally returned back to Vancouver, B.C, Canada, it was the first week of March and David was recovering from his second round of chemotherapy. It was then and there that I realized just how much he was downplaying his condition. He posted mainly positive remarks

CHAPTER TWO: David's Dream

on Face book, usually with pictures of himself smiling and his muscles flexed. No one really knew the truth of the little time he had left, and how sick he really was, except Rolf and I, my parents, and some of my dad's siblings. We also expressed the truth of what had been revealed through my blessing to Rolf's daughter Mohna. I felt Kristen somehow just knew the truth. It seemed like most everyone else in the family did not want to know the truth or talk about it much. I was glad I could share my feelings with my husband, who was most supportive. It was especially hard when David would talk about his future plans, including a possible marriage to his girlfriend Kristen.

David fought to live and tried not only chemotherapy and radiation, but also a device called a "photon genie," which distributes light energy and is known to help cancer patients. Unfortunately, the photon genie did not even touch David's kind of cancer. David regularly took vitamins and drank fruit juices and smoothies his sister Laura so kindly made for him. Laura came all the way from Missouri to Canada with her family to help support David. At first, Laura would only accept the idea that we were going to make David better, and did not want to think about or talk about any other outcome. I had a lot on my hands because I knew what the Lord had revealed to me, and I could not deny it. I wished that I might be wrong; hoping he still had years left, but deep down knew this was not the case.

We started seeing the side effects of these treatments when we returned for a long span of time in early March, after his first treatments at B.C Children's Hospital. He had very dark circles around his eyes from the chemotherapy treatments, and bright red burns where they had radiated his hip and groin area. He slept a lot and would often fall asleep, even when carrying on the simplest of conversations. He had a venous port inserted under the surface skin of his right chest making it easier to not only receive chemotherapy, but also a constant stream of medication. He had decided to shave his head after a few treatments of chemotherapy. I think he still wanted to have some control over his circumstances.

This was the first time I saw David bald, but he still looked ever so cute! We stayed in Ronald McDonald house on this particular visit. David had been given permission to stay in a hospice called, "Canuck Place." This special care facility looked like a miniature palace! It had four spacious floors, including the basement area. On the third floor there were four family suites that were adorned with beautiful stained glass windows. We were able to stay close to David in Canuck Place soon after our stay in Ronald McDonald house.

CHAPTER TWO: David's Dream

(Canuck Place in Vancouver, B.C Canada)

    There was a piano in the family sitting area, in which I enjoyed playing on regularly. David sang here with me on a couple of occasions. The last song we sang together was "Abide with Me Tis Eventide." We had sung it together on many occasions before. Singing, though, did become quite difficult for David once he began these treatments. There was a room for games and a craft area on this floor as well. On the second floor there were private beds and bathrooms for about eight patients at a time and each patient had his or her own nurse.

    A beautiful hand carved staircase led from the first floor to the third. On the first floor there was a friendly receptionist who sat in front of two rooms. One room consisted of air hockey, video games, and a large dollhouse. The other room was comprised of couches, tables, and chairs for meetings, massages, and performances. We were given the opportunity of receiving massage, free of charge every Friday,

15

Be Still My Soul

and grief counseling as often as we needed. Canuck Place was a haven for terminally ill children and teens, and besides professional staff, there were also many volunteers working to uplift each patient.

To the right of these fabulous rooms was the family eating, serving and kitchen area. The most delicious meals were prepared and served here three times a day.

David gained over thirty pounds while eating the food at Canuck Place, also with the help of Dexamethasone, a steroid that gave him a raging appetite. This medicine gave David his cute "moonfaced look," as he so often called it; however, it was only a temporary reaction. He made friends, even with the nurses and staff members, who loved him dearly. Two of his close friends, Gabby and Patrick,

CHAPTER TWO: David's Dream

among others, passed away while David was still being nurtured at Canuck Place. These were hard, yet tender moments for us all.

David had fun playing monopoly with the many volunteers who came daily, and usually was the winner. I've managed to beat David at monopoly on a few occasions, but only once at Canuck Place. He set up monopoly tournaments with the volunteers who came to see him daily. He also performed a song or two for volunteers when he was able. David had many visitors, including the Prime Minister of British Columbia, Christy Clark, who briefly spoke with him one day when she visited the patients at Canuck Place. This opened up the opportunity for David to be seen on national television!

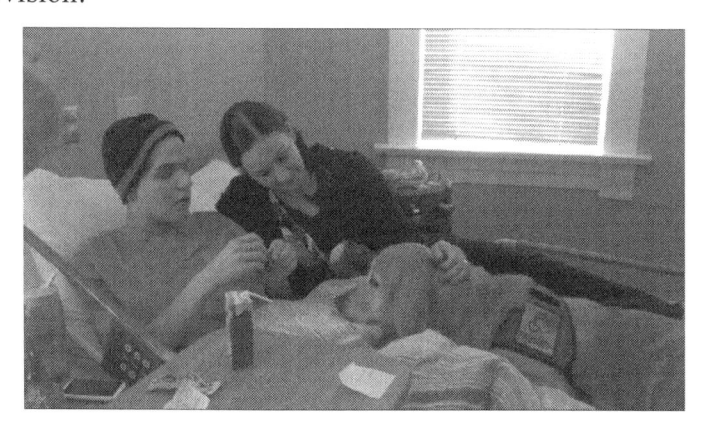

David was regularly visited by a therapy dog named "Poppy" who was so loving and gentle. She would lay herself down on David's bed and sympathetically stare at him, always wanting a hug herself. She made her rounds to all the patients and was most welcome.

David went on quite a few shopping trips to the mall for new clothes, usually by shuttle, while staying at Canuck Place. He was especially concerned about looking good for his dream trip to Las Vegas.

We went along, usually with a nurse, on a few of these excursions to make sure he didn't overdo it. One afternoon of shopping usually meant one to two days of sleeping the next. Nurses and staff members also took patients to free movies by shuttle, and we were invited to go along with David as we pleased. The Easterbrooks were very generous by taking us out to the movies with David on a few occasions as well. David usually had a smile, and always a kind word to say about everyone.

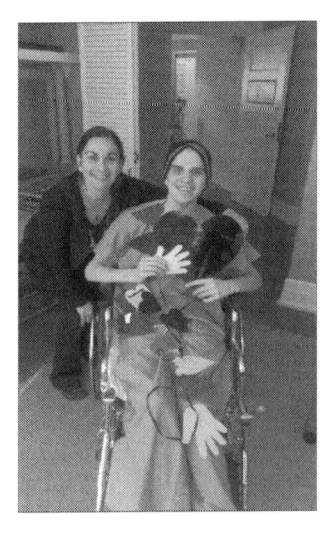

CHAPTER TWO: David's Dream

Rolf and I presented David with a string of hearts from those who had so generously donated to his dream trip to Las Vegas. Candy Burton set up an online site for donations, which was very successful. Enough money was donated for David's flight, a two night's stay in Caesar's palace, and Celine Dion tickets. I was anxiously waiting to hear back from Debbie Osmond at this time. My prayers were answered in early March, when Debbie announced that they had finally got an affirmative response that David could meet Celine privately. We were all just as thrilled as he was! We invited Kristen, his girl friend, to come with us too. Rolf and I traveled by car back home first to get Kristen, and then on to Las Vegas. David's father flew with him from Canada to meet up with us. David's neck was beginning to hurt by this time due to the cancer metastasizing into his neck, and was told that these tumors were also inoperable.

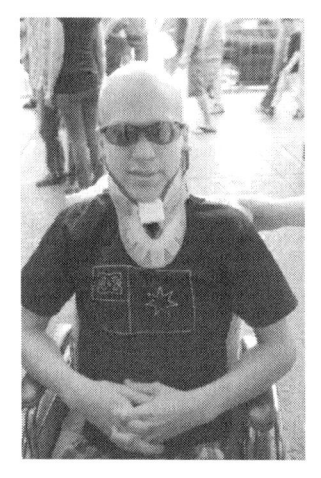

David was informed he was to wear a sturdy neck brace most of the time if he was to go on this Vegas trip. He looked quite different, but still cute, with his bald head, sunglasses and stiff neck brace. He told me when he met up with us in Las Vegas that it had been necessary for him to have a blood transfusion before going. I remember being extremely worried if he would have the strength to hold out and earnestly prayed he would be able to make it through. He had to constantly shoot himself with an assortment of medications and adhere Fentanyl patches to his arms for extra relief, which kept him fairly comfortable most of the time. His left leg and hands were shaking most of the time, but he was elated to have been able to go. David was basically confined to a wheelchair by this time.

Kristen, Rolf and I met him in the Las Vegas airport and enjoyed visiting and shopping with him that first day. Some of David's friends from Provo and Las Vegas met up with us, sometimes even in our hotel room at Caesar's Palace, due to him being on heavy medication. David also wanted to see "The Donny and Marie Show." I mentioned this to Debbie Osmond, so she could schedule great seats for us. This was to take place on the last night we were in Vegas.

We were informed upon arrival in Vegas that we were to meet up with Celine just before her show the next evening. When we were greeted by her, David was so moved and cried out loud when she took him into her arms! We all were so emotionally touched by this and wept ourselves. She compassionately told him that she knew they would meet again someday. I knew she meant heaven, and then told David, "I will be singing for you tonight!"

CHAPTER TWO: David's Dream

Kristen, David and I were given great seats closer up front, while his father, and my husband Rolf, took their seats farther away. To watch his enthusiasm meant a lot to me. He was totally enthralled! He wanted to spend time with Kristen that first night, so we waited and worried as she wheeled him around to some of the sights of Las Vegas. I was concerned that he would be too tired the next night for "The Donny and Marie Show," but he wisely slept most of that day so he could make it. When we finally got to the Flamingo the next evening, Debbie Osmond greeted us and lead us back stage to be with them all. They treated us like family as we visited and took pictures before and after the show.

Share David's Dream Event: Flamingo Resort Showroom Backstage With Donny, Marie and Debby Osmond © 2013 Cate Vail/ SirensPhotography / PR Photos

Marie also showed up to make a fuss over David backstage. During the show, she came up, plastered her lips with heavy red lipstick, and kissed his bald head! She always kissed the bald men on top of their heads during the show and David was her last target that night.

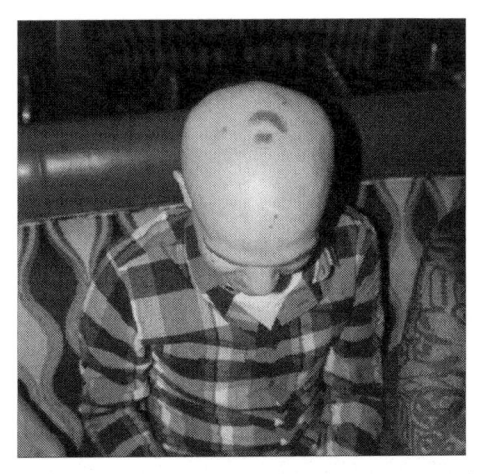

We shall never forget the Osmond's generosity, care and concern for David. They applied the commandment of loving your neighbor as yourself; they truly were amazing. It was only the start of the attention they provided for David. As busy as they can be, Donny and Debbie came to visit David at our home before his passing, and then came to his funeral in

CHAPTER TWO: David's Dream

August of 2013. My sister, Catherine Vail, met up with us to enjoy these shows as well. She is a great photographer and took the concert and backstage photos of us with the Osmonds.

(Cate Vail with David backstage in the Osmond's dressing room)

(Kristen and David backstage in Donny's dressing room)

(David backstage with Donny & Debby Osmond)

Be Still My Soul

(Emily Adair with David on Vegas Strip)

(Emma Smith with David)

(Rosalie Spears with David)

(David with the Spears family in Henderson, Nevada)

CHAPTER THREE: Ups and Downs

"My son, peace be unto thy soul; thine adversity and thine afflictions shall be but a small moment; and then if thou endure it well, God shall exalt thee on high; thou shalt triumph over all thy foes." [1]

The next day, we drove Kristen home with us to Provo, before leaving soon afterwards to Canada. David flew back with his father, on a nonstop flight to Vancouver, so he could once again be admitted into B.C Children's Hospital for another round of radiation and chemotherapy. It was crucial to keep these treatments consistent, in hopes of slowing down the growth of tumors that were aggressively metastasizing. When we returned back to Canada, David was already at Canuck Place recovering from six days of treatments. When we rushed into his hospice room, it was quite apparent the treatments had taken a heavy toll on his energy. He slept almost continuously with little sustenance for about a week. David started gaining strength within two weeks and was able to associate with us again.

He spoke of his great Vegas trip, but how he now was missing Kristen so terribly. He told me he loved her and that they would probably get married in the near future. It was hardest for me when he was not realizing the Lord's will. I struggled to express my feelings openly not wanting to upset him or anyone else. It was no easy task to help prepare him for what lay ahead, mainly because of his constant pain and the many distractions of the world. I lived off of prayer! It was a very stressful time for me with always knowing it to be my responsibility to prepare him for his passing.

By early April, my stepdaughter, Mohna, who resides in Inkom, Idaho, a tiny town just situated outside of Pocatello, took the journey by car with her boys, Caleb, Josh and Andrew to visit David in Vancouver at Canuck Place. Mohna and David are quite similar in personality. She is extremely thoughtful and considerate and knows how to compassionately put herself in another's shoes. She first visited the children and their families on Vancouver Island, giving David time to recover from these last treatments.

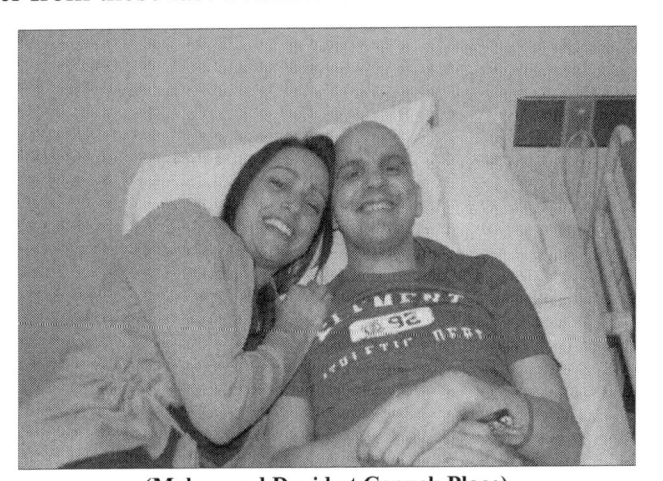

(Mohna and David at Canuck Place)

They came to Canuck Place at a very opportune time. A few former Canuck team players came to visit the patients while they were with us. They all had a blast meeting former team members and painting their shirts in vibrant colors.

CHAPTER THREE: Ups and Downs

(Former Canuck team player with Josh and Caleb Thuernagle)

(Caleb, Josh and Andrew Thuernagle)

Mohna and the boys also spent a few days playing board games, watching movies and uplifting David.

David felt the need to reprove one of our grandsons for ignoring his mother's requests on the last night they were visiting us. It didn't take much to convince David to remember to show forth much love after such a reprimand. He took him aside and had a very crucial discussion with him the next morning. David had a special way with people; they always knew how much he cared for and loved them, even when he

27

may have disapproved of their actions. He exemplified the characteristics of charity, "Charity is kind, not easily provoked, thinketh no evil, and rejoiceth not in iniquity but rejoiceth in the truth."[2] I was elated they had departed on such loving terms.

About this time, David decided to buy a ring for Kristen and insisted on going to Utah to propose. This was clearly impossible with the terrible side effects he was experiencing. His radiation treatments had caused a fissure to develop making elimination a most excruciating experience. David asked me what it had been like having a baby "naturally," and then agreed his bathroom experiences were similar in pain intensity. It was a tremendous ordeal for him to go, sometimes taking days, as he breathed in nitrous oxide to help him relax enough to muster up the courage to get through the screaming torture!

Sandy Hodge, one of David's favorite nurses at Canuck Place, was always so caring and compassionate, especially during these torturous times. She became a close friend to David, and he enjoyed her personality immensely. I noticed, on a few occasions, him talking with her deeply about his beliefs. David tried to closely follow the principles and teachings of The Church of Jesus Christ of Latter-day Saints and had a testimony of its truthfulness. He enjoyed sharing his understanding of life and always put things in simple terms, so he could relate to most everyone.

CHAPTER THREE: Ups and Downs

(Sandy Hodge with David outside of Canuck Place)

David decided to receive a priesthood blessing in hopes of overcoming his fear of using the bathroom. After a much needed blessing, which his father gave to him, David was able to finally relax enough to go after countless days of holding back. His fissure started to heal quickly, which increased his faith, but those giving him blessings never felt inspired to tell him he would be healed from the cancer. We stayed at Canuck Place for more than three weeks due to this terrible fissure.

About this time, Kristen was having second thoughts about coming to live in the Vancouver area as David had wished. Kristen loved David dearly, but was just not ready to make the commitment of living there. This caused great pain for David because marriage seemed out of the question at this point. Because of his unconditional love for her, he told her he understood, and tried to let go of the idea of getting married. This is the kind of person David was; always putting other's needs and feelings before his own, even when under enormous stress and pain.

CHAPTER FOUR: As I Have Loved You

"A new commandment I give unto you, that ye love one another, as I have loved you, that ye also love one another." 1

Kristen decided to come for a ten day visit in May. Just before this time, David's fissure was healed enough for him to go, by ambulance, into the palliative unit of the Nanaimo Hospital so he could be closer to the rest of the family. We followed along closely by car. Kristen met up with us soon after his arrival. Most of the time while she visited, David slept. It was around this time that David started to realize that his past treatments were not helping much to improve his situation. Further X-rays showed that the cancer had not improved much. He was thrilled, however, for new bone growth in his hip, making it easier to stand for short periods of time. Even though he and Kristen were not going to get married, David still gave her the ring he had chosen and a few other gifts. He looked like a different person with thirty pounds of weight gain, and no hair or eyebrows!

Be Still My Soul

I was torn about going back to Utah in May because I knew he was getting closer to the end, but I also knew my mother needed my love, especially at this time for Mother's Day. I've never forgotten the look on my son's face upon leaving. He was really starting to show signs of emotional stress, so I told him I would return soon. I cried most of the way home knowing that I could not ever leave him again. I did, though, have a wonderful visit as I spent precious time with my mother. When we returned in less than a week, it was close to the end of May.

We learned that while we had been away, David had been refused chemotherapy due to extreme weakness. Actually I was relieved; I did not get a good feeling about him having another full dose. He was able to finally move into his room in the basement of the house his dad had helped buy for my daughter Laura and her family. Laura and her husband Matthew so kindly renovated a downstairs bedroom and bathroom for David. Laura painted his room with fancy keyboards running down as borders along the wall corners. In one corner of the room, she even included the Monopoly Man! He had a large stack of junk food; including "Twizzlers", "Pop Tarts", "Ramen", and chocolate bars. Laura wanted to please him, but tried hard to get him to consistently take healthy smoothies and vitamins, as well use his photon genie. Laura was like a mother to David for much of his growing up years, and enjoyed mothering him once again. David and Laura had a

CHAPTER FOUR: As I Have Loved You

very close, loving bond throughout the years. Laura's husband Matthew and her children, Matty Jr. and Benton also adored David.

(David with Sister Laura Alms)

Anna, his oldest sister, also did some mothering of her own. She took lots of time off at work to be with him. I was pleased when she brought movies, doughnuts, "Scratch and Wins", or any other thing he may be craving. Her family played a variety of games with David, including "Monopoly". I was very grateful for her help, especially when she came over to Vancouver to visit, uplift and to support him. It was harder for the other family members to come regularly when he was in Vancouver because they had small children to tend to. Her son Alex was eleven years old at the time and usually came along with her husband Ryan to be with David. Alex so thoughtfully made David a special pillow with the words colored, "Be strong!" They all loved David immensely.

(David with Sister Anna Chow)

David had a collection of sixteen Monopoly games. He got to play almost all of them at least once or twice. He loved <u>Harry Potter</u> and bought the whole edition to read again, even though he had read them through on so many occasions before. He use to have "Harry Potter read a-thons" with friends in years past. I was glad David had disability money so he could shop for fun stuff once in awhile. David loved "Timbits" doughnuts from Tim Horton's, "Twizzlers" licorice, "Slurpees", oatmeal cookies with marshmallow middles, and Thai food. One could find him nibbling on these treats up until the time he lost his appetite before his bodily functions shut down. He also loved ice cream, and ate it by the ton! I knew these junk foods aggravated the cancer, but these treats brought him satisfaction, and with knowing how little time he had left, I wanted him to enjoy these simple pleasures as long as he was able.

CHAPTER FOUR: As I Have Loved You

Chris, David's older brother, also visited whenever he could find the time. He was extremely busy with a demanding job, being elder's quorum president, running after his two year old twin daughters, and supporting his pregnant wife, Laura, who was soon to deliver their third daughter. Chris loved his little brother David dearly. I appreciated that he took time off work to be with him towards the end, and also appreciated his willingness to give blessings, and the sacrament to David on Sundays. His wife Laura, including Isabelle and Abigail, had a loving relationship with David.

(Laura, Isabelle, Abigail and Chris Gow)

CHAPTER FIVE: Trusting In the Lord

"Trust in the lord with all thine heart; and lean not unto thine own understanding" 1

David got permission to take a small dose of chemotherapy at the end of May, and then was admitted into Canuck Place again for ten days. This was the last time David stayed there. This particular recovery was an especially difficult one, because David also experienced depression after getting the news that the chemotherapy treatments were not doing much to stop the cancer from growing. With the terrible side effects he was experiencing from these treatments, it just didn't seem worth it to continue. He then made the difficult decision, to stop chemotherapy altogether. It was then that he came to the acceptance that he may not have the time left he had hoped for.

David had always accepted the fact that eventually the cancer could take over, but he had no idea how quickly. David always thought he may have years left, or at least hoped so. It was a difficult time for him, especially with being only nineteen years old, to accept that his time here in mortality was almost over. I had been so impressed with his courage and how he wanted to fight, even under extremely painful circumstances. But I was glad when he made the decision to finally stop the poison that was not making much of a difference, and only prolonging his suffering.

Be Still My Soul

We called a special family meeting with the nursing staff and a few doctors, so he could have his wishes written down. His father also joined into the discussion long distance by speaker phone. His father had to make continuous trips back and forth from Vanderhoof to Vancouver because he hadn't completely retired from his teaching job and still had loose ends to tie up in Vanderhoof. At this meeting, David gave me permission to make future decisions for him once he became incapable. This was an especially sad time for us all. We knew once he stopped the therapy, the cancer would spread even faster. I was relieved though that he had come to an understanding that he didn't have a long time left, which made it much easier for me to help him prepare emotionally and spiritually. Angiosarcoma isn't like most cancers that can be slowed down through operation and healthy choices. It grew mercilessly and it had been progressing even with rigorous treatment. As sad as it was knowing it wouldn't be long before we would have to say goodbye, I was extremely relieved that it would now be apparent to everyone how little time he had left. I was able to muster up the courage to speak frankly with David from then on. There was still so much to say and do to prepare him for his passing.

David decided to return to his room in Nanaimo by early June. He never failed to show courage and tried to make the most of the time he had left. He felt the need to go to Utah as soon as he was able. He wanted, once more, to visit with his

CHAPTER FIVE: Trusting In the Lord

grandparents, friends, past ward members, and of course Kristen. His fissure was completely healed just before we decided to take him on June 26th, the day after his sister Laura's birthday. We planned many fun activities together as a family before our departure.

We had a room, which was located near our cabin at Westwood Lake that we reserved for family activities. Rolf and I took long hikes around the lake quite often. Being together often helped us grow closer together as a family. Through the Lord's help, we were able to clear up a past misunderstanding that had caused much division in the family. This had been quite a miracle and I knew David had been pleased with us, and amazed himself. God is never happy with disharmony and division; especially in families. I know the Lord was pleased with our efforts. At this time, my daughter Laura was able to finally accept and understand, through the Lord's help, why David was being called to the other side. This will be explained later on, but it brought such joy to me to see her finally at peace.

Be Still My Soul

(David Gow, Helen and Rolf Bertler, Laura, Matthew, Matty and Benton Alms, Anna Chow, Alex Beausouli, and Ryan Chow)

(Family time in the Westwood activity room)

(Family Pool time with Alex, Anna and Laura)

CHAPTER SIX: Mighty Miracles

"Yea, I know that I am nothing; as to my strength I am weak: therefore I will not boast of myself, but I will boast of my God, for in his strength I can do all things; yea, behold many mighty miracles we have wrought in this land, for which we will praise his name forever."[1]

Traveling back to Utah was no easy task with David's need for "around the clock care," but we really desired to fulfill this special wish of his. We prayed fervently and trusted in the Lord to make it happen. We were able get David safely to our motel room on the way to Utah where my husband filled syringes for injections. We looked like junkies with tons of syringes and needles spread across our motel room! It is illegal to take filled syringes across the border, so we filled a few after crossing and then prepared enough in our motel room to be used for three days. Without these medications, David would have gone insane with pain!

We had accepted the possibility that David could die on this trip, and made prayer a regular occurrence in hopes he could make it back to Canada so his brother, sisters, and father would still have time left to share with him. David was quite comfortable in his seat that went back far enough to keep him fairly relaxed while traveling. That night in our motel room, David had a dream which caused him to sing aloud in his sleep. It had been quite a treat to hear him sing once again, which was the last live performance we were privileged to hear from him.

41

Be Still My Soul

We did not tell my parents we were coming because we were uncertain if we would be able to make it. We did not want to cause worry or disappointment if somehow we had to turn back. God made our travels very comfortable on the way. David never complained about pain and even visited with us on occasion, sharing his deep feelings and thoughts. He had some questions he wanted to take up with my father when he got to Provo. At that time he was still hoping for a miracle, but he was confused about a few things in his Patriarchal Blessing, which we tried to help him come to grips with.

What an enormous surprise it was for my parents to have the opportunity to be with David again. My mother cried out loud; when she realized it was David who had been hiding around the corner when we took them down to eat in the dining hall at Courtyard at Jamestown the evening we got there!

It was difficult to tell how much pain David was experiencing because he had become incredibly tough from being in such severe pain for almost a year. His neck was in a

CHAPTER SIX: Mighty Miracles

brace again. It must have hurt greatly, but he didn't complain much as we traveled. His leg was fairly comfortable as long as he faithfully accepted the medications that Rolf administered to him, which still consisted of Ketorolac, Hydromorphone, Methadone and Fentanyl patches. His doctor had given us an extra drug called Ketamine because the other drugs were not giving him enough relief anymore. It was quite a miracle we made this trip because in the past he could have never traveled by car; especially with all his bad side effects from past treatments.

David had many visitors in Provo, especially after I announced at church that he was at our house visiting for a short period of time. It was another tender mercy from the Lord to have him visit with so many, friends, family, and ward members, including our Stake President. It was like having a ten day missionary farewell open house! My friends told me they had felt angels in our house, and indeed there were many, from this side of the veil as well as the other. While in Utah, David was only able to get out of bed on a few occasions. He went on two short excursions with Kristen; one being on the 4th of July.

These fun activities with Kristen were the last David was able to experience on his own. He told me how enjoyable it had been to go out again. I remember being in disbelief how long he stayed out to have fun on the 4th of July. I again had the opportunity of worrying as I waited up for him. It was another little gift from the Lord! Debbie and Donny Osmond paid him a short, special visit the next evening, which was most tender and memorable.

(Kristen and David on the 4th of July)

The next day my father gave David a blessing, in which he was told how much the Lord loved him, and how wonderful his next life would be. This gave David much comfort because he was somewhat confused about his patriarchal blessing. It was revealed to him that the Lord had a very special mission for him; one in which he will be able to bring others to the gospel of Jesus Christ, and he would have greater opportunities to significantly use his musical talents to help others on the other side of the veil. He was also promised that all the blessings in his Patriarchal Blessing would come true, including marriage and family,

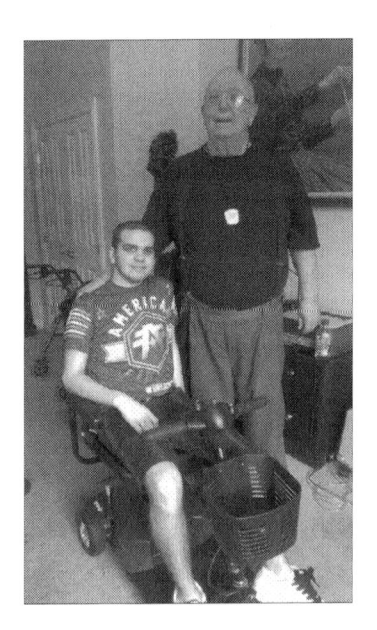

CHAPTER SIX: Mighty Miracles

during the millennium after his resurrection. He also was told that he would be able to make choices in doing things he desired and these choices would bring him much joy. I knew this blessing brought him much peace and understanding.

The Lord has so much in store for us; more than we can ever imagine or hope for. I know any blessings that may not be recognized in this life will be granted beyond our expectations in the next. President Joseph F. Smith, one of our past beloved prophets of the Church of Jesus Christ of Latter day Saints exclaimed, "Joseph Smith declared, the mother who laid down her little child, being deprived of the privilege, the joy and the satisfaction of bringing it up to manhood or womanhood in this world, would, after the resurrection, have all the joy, satisfaction and pleasure, *and even more than it would have been possible to have had in mortality*, in seeing her child grow to the full measure of the stature of its spirit."[2] This is such comforting doctrine, to know that I will enjoy watching David grow fully to his stature as a priesthood holder during the millennium, and then have the privilege of watching the blessings of marriage and children come true, even to a fuller extent than it would have been in this lifetime! We just need to be righteous enough to earn this reward by loving and serving our fellowmen, living the commandments, and repenting when we fall short.

I am so grateful Jesus atoned for my sins, after all I can do. Jesus took up the slack for us all, but God expects us to still exert our heart and soul into becoming more obedient to his will. David was told he should prepare for his passing by reading the scriptures and praying often, and if he did these things he would feel the Lord's love more deeply. David had trouble reading, even for short periods of time, so I decided to start reading with him. We started in 3 Nephi, since he had never studied that part of the Book of Mormon before. There was always a peaceful feeling when I engaged in these activities with him.

Towards the end of our visit in Provo, David was again starting to have tremendous pain down his left leg, even with extra doses of medication. It was a very stressful time because we were away from his doctor and care in Canada. We received permission from Dr. Love in Canada, who always answered immediately when we tried to reach him, to decrease the length of duration between his doses of medication. His doctor was a great help on this trip, even though he was far away in Nanaimo. I've always considered his insight to be inspired.

David had trouble sleeping in Utah and fought for relief continuously night after night with little sleep. We ran to his aid constantly in the day, but he didn't want to bother us at night, so groaned quietly to not wake us too early. I would wake up to find him trying to deal with the pain on his own. This was how considerate David was, even when under extreme pain and agony. We again prayed his pain would be

CHAPTER SIX: Mighty Miracles

manageable on the way home.

I was in tears with worry about our travel back home, especially because we had misplaced the papers that gave us permission to take narcotics over the border. I had to take Valium so I could relax enough to be able to travel through the night. My friend Eva Herrey, and our neighbor Sharon Kennedy were so comforting to me before we headed back to Canada. The cancerous tumor in his leg was growing and pressing upon his sciatic nerve again. Just before we left for Canada, I remembered that Percocet had helped me tremendously when I had sciatic pain due to a past operation.

We felt inspired to find this medicine, which was stored somewhere in the clutter of our disorganized house. We desperately begged for the Lord's help! Within a minute, the bag which contained this medicine literally fell off the dresser in front of us. It was hiding underneath some things making it hard to spot. I knew this was not by accident, angels were constantly helping us. We are promised in the scriptures, "I will go before your face. I will be on your right hand and on your left and my spirit shall be in your hearts, and mine angels round about you, to bear you up."[3] We surely felt this promise.

Rolf administered the Percocet to David just before attempting our journey. We had just enough Percocet to get him through the night. He slept for the first time in a week. I usually cannot sleep in a moving car and suffer from road anxiety, but was able to sleep while traveling for the first time in years; another great miracle. My husband was also blessed to tirelessly drive, almost nonstop, until the morning. I was grateful Rolf had not revealed to me that one of our tires was having serious issues in the middle of the night. My husband took it slowly to avoid a disaster.

We safely made it to the Washington area by morning, where we had our tire serviced immediately and quickly. It was then that I became increasingly worried about our misplaced papers that gave permission for us to take narcotics over the border. To avoid trouble, we decided to not mention that we were carrying a terminally ill passenger. This was not a wise choice for it did not give border security a reason to overlook why we were carrying so many belongings. Security made us pull over and questioned us, trying to make David get out of the car until they realized just how sick he was. I told them that he was terminally ill and we needed to get on our way as soon as possible. I was glad when they said, "You should have mentioned this in the first place." I then got nervous thinking they may ask about medications and papers, but they never did. I was very grateful, but this experience had slowed us down and we had a ferry to catch!

I petitioned the Lord again for another miracle. My husband relentlessly sped through traffic in hopes of catching the next ferry. Most of the terminals were closed by the time we arrived, but we noticed an "open" sign still flashing as the last cars were moving on. When we drove up, a lady ran up to

CHAPTER SIX: Mighty Miracles

exclaim "I forgot to turn my open sign off," but let us go through anyway, just in time! We practically drove right on before the gate closed up, being the last car to make it. I knew my prayers had been answered once again.

David decided to stay down in our car below deck, mainly due to extreme exhaustion. Rolf and I quickly went to grab a bite. When we returned, we found David suffering again, but now with electrifying stabs of pain, which relentlessly coursed through his tumorous leg. Rolf had no choice but to shoot him with an extra dose of Ketamine. David disliked taking it because it caused him to helplessly hallucinate. With his pain becoming increasingly unmanageable, David decided to take it anyways. He saw strange shapes and textures as he spoke senselessly, but the drug worked to calm his soul as well as mine. I knew his doctor had been inspired to give us this drug before leaving; we also had to give it to him on a few occasions in Provo.

After we landed on Vancouver Island, we flew at top speed, like an ambulance on an emergency, directly to the Nanaimo hospital, where a bed was waiting for him. The hospital was only a ten minute drive from the Departure Bay Ferry Terminal. A few nurses met us at the entrance of the palliative unit to quickly help him crawl into a comfortable hospital bed. It was the 10th of July on this miraculous day. I thanked my Heavenly Father for all the miracles we had experienced in getting David safely to Utah and back.

CHAPTER SEVEN: Be Still My Soul

"Did I not speak peace to your mind concerning the matter? What greater witness can you have than from God?"1

When we admitted David into the hospital, different nurses tried various techniques to get his horrific leg pain under control. After a few frustrating days, it was decided to put him on an intrathecal pump to help him get a more efficient flow of his medications. These medications just didn't seem to be working to give him enough relief anymore. Rolf and I nervously waited in a room close by; we were willing to try almost anything for his relief by this point. When he came out of the insertion procedure, I noticed him to have a look of shock imprinted upon his face. I did feel thankful, though, that we had found something to increase his chances of relief, which he unfortunately didn't immediately experience.

The pump did not work to give enough relief at first. It was a new procedure, which even his doctors had trouble getting to work effectively. I was concerned and stayed close by David's side every night in the hospital from that time forward. Very early the next morning, David had an extremely outrageous reaction. He compared this reaction to being eaten alive by tingly, itchy ants! I've never felt so helpless in my life. Whatever we tried did not bring him relief. Even the nurses were at a loss in how to help him. He screamed for it to be taken out! I held him in my arms, as we cried together. I

Be Still My Soul

pleaded again to God that he would soon find relief!

I asked my oldest son Chris, who was on an early morning work shift, if he could come to give David a blessing. Unfortunately, due to the lack of staff support at such an early hour, he was not able to come. I then desperately called my husband over and over again. He had gone to our cabin that night to catch up on some sleep. When I finally reached him, I begged for him to come quickly to give David a blessing. I knew my pleadings had been heard because within a few minutes after I got off the phone with my husband, the doctor who had inserted David's pump, burst into the room from another emergency, to freeze David from the waist down. The freezing worked within minutes to calm him down. I was close to a nervous breakdown myself. Rolf came soon after to bless David with peace. He also blessed David's equipment to work efficiently. The pump finally did work with only one minor problem from that time forward. David received much relief from this pump, but was confined to bed due to his frozen extremities. He finally was pain free in his left leg for the first time in months. I was thankful to the Lord for helping us find again what we needed to do to help bring him more relief.

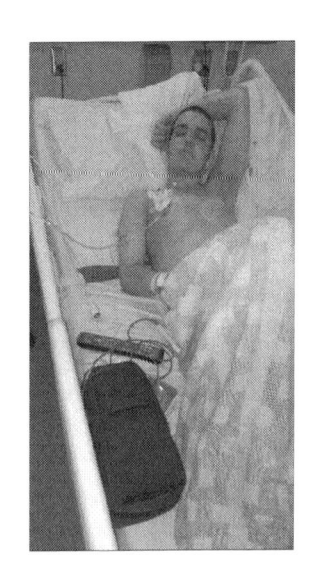

CHAPTER SEVEN: Be Still My Soul

Unfortunately his neck could not be frozen. He had to take extra doses of Methadone for relief of the growing tumors that were now invading the blood vessels in his neck. We put his neck in such a position as to not put too much pressure on the obvious bulge that was protruding by this time. He was changed and cleaned frequently for he was helpless by this time in the middle of July, but was in good spirits with being able to finally sleep after such a long period of time. David enjoyed visiting and playing handheld electronic games for a time. His sister Laura bought him a mini Game boy. He couldn't do much but watch TV, listen as we read, play on his Game boy or text and talk to the occasional friend on Face book. He still did not inform his friends of his helpless predicament.

I was taken by surprise, when a doctor approached me one morning to show me a picture of his lungs. The x-ray showed how the cancer had spread so widely. I got nervous knowing that it would just be a matter of days before he would struggle to breathe. David asked me to take a picture of the x-ray so he could come to terms with the little time he had left. We both knew then that shortly his lungs would collapse. I do remember, though, being grateful I had listened to the early promptings warning me he didn't have a lot of time left in mortality, which had caused me to borrow as much time as I could with him.

We were able to talk about many important things

before he went under sedation. Together, with his sister Laura, we decided the order of the songs for his CD. He was thrilled we were going to make one to give away to everyone! I asked David if he could fulfill one simple wish for me, which was to sing in my ear when he got to the other side so I would know he was ok. He agreed. He also requested a few wishes for his funeral, which included my public testimony. I agreed.

To everyone's surprise, David asked if he could be buried in Provo, Utah. I thought he somehow had read my mind, for I did not ever vocally tell him I desired this or expected it because most of the family is situated in Canada. I felt spoiled that I would be able to visit his grave often, but felt he especially wanted to give this gift to Kristen his sweetheart. He wrote a special goodbye letter to her and insisted that it be mailed immediately before he went under sedation. She told me she got it soon after she returned home after his passing, and how it had lifted her spirit so much. David's timing was impeccable; he always knew what to say to uplift others at the right moment.

We should never take anyone for granted, especially our loved ones. No one can tell for sure how long they will have the privilege of being with a loved one in this lifetime. Every moment had been precious with David and we had spent our time with him to the fullest. I know that demonstrating unconditional love and spending quality time together as a family is of the utmost importance in God's eyes.

CHAPTER SEVEN: Be Still My Soul

I felt impressed to leave my church meetings one of the last Sundays David was still with us. I knew I was to have a gospel discussion with him that day. We'd had a wonderful conversation the day before, as I told him of personal experiences how reading the Book of Mormon had helped me in my life. I felt that he was very open at this time to having deep conversations because his pain was finally under control. This Sunday morning, when I reached his room, I found him playing on his "Game boy". I felt prompted to ask him to put it away so I could teach him a priesthood lesson that I had found on obedience. He politely put away his game to listen.

One of the nurses asked if she could help roll his bed outside in the courtyard with it being a beautiful day. He agreed that it would be nice to go outside. The nurses, doctors, including Dr. Pritchard and Dr. Love, counselors and volunteers in the Nanaimo Palliative Unit, Canuck Place and B.C Children's Hospital were like close friends to David and our family, and we loved them dearly. They did an awesome job in taking care of our David. We have been most grateful for their loving care.

When David and I got outside, I talked with him about what it truly means to honor the priesthood. He was very attentive and basically pain free; a situation that was usually impossible. We both were incredibly blessed and talked deeply for almost three hours. It was one of the best, if not best, teaching moments I have ever had with my son, and it was also the last! It had been quite a miracle that we had been able to talk with no disruptions, another wonderful gift from the Lord that I hold most dear. I felt peace after our discussion and knew David understood and had a strong testimony of the Gospel of Jesus Christ, and had accepted the Lord's will for his future. Everyone needed to be with him, which took up all of his time from then on. Chris and Rolf brought him the sacrament later that day.

Two days later, David started feeling pain in his chest and a tickly throat. The doctor explained to me that he was very close to having his lungs fail and would start to suffocate soon. I never anticipated such horrific things for my son to have to pass through! Coughing is a common symptom when the lungs start to collapse, and David did plenty of it. By looking at him, I could tell his internal organs were also starting to shut down. When I was concerned he wasn't eating anymore, he calmly reassured me, "Mom, this is just part of the process." His calmness always brought such comfort to me.

CHAPTER EIGHT: David, Our Beloved

"Yea though I walk through the valley of the shadow of death, I will fear no evil; for thou art with me; thy rod and thy staff they comfort me"1

One of David's doctors heard that we were planning an early birthday party for him and asked when it was to happen. After learning the date, the doctor urgently persuaded me to move it up a few days. I also felt strongly to go buy the "Mac book Pro" laptop he had always wanted, so he could experience the joy of using it, even if it was just for a short time.

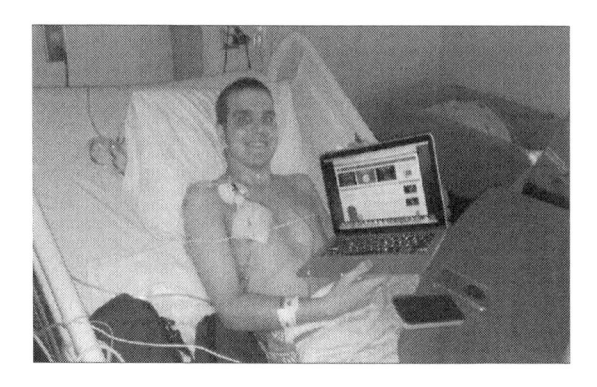

The first thing he did was "Face Time" Kristen on it. He thought it cool to own one, and enjoyed a good part of that day playing on it. I was extremely glad I had acted upon this prompting because it ended up being the only day he had the strength to use it; that night his lungs starting shutting down.

The night just before this happened, I had asked his father, and his sister Laura if they could sleep in his room so I could catch up on some sleep nearby. My husband and I stayed in the family room down the hall nearby. After we arose and came into his room the next morning, we heard about his breathing attack, and that his father was now in the emergency room due to his own panic attack from watching his son suffer. After this first episode, David had to keep a full breathing mask on constantly. The nurses gave David his first sedation at this time, which caused him to sleep a good part of that day. I was relieved I had told everyone the party was to be at 3PM. David was able to wake up just in time for the party, but was drowsy. I know he enjoyed being with us, but was quite sober from his experiences.

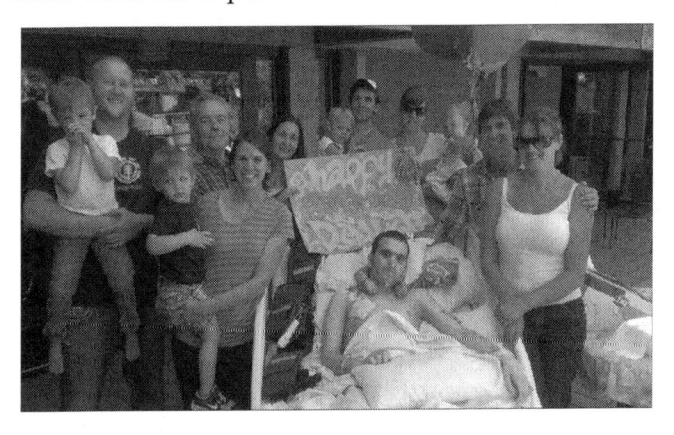

All of the children and their families came to his birthday party. The Easterbrooks also came with their son, who had made a special birthday poster for David. My good friend Leanne Hughes also came with her husband to offer love and support for us all. She has the greatest listening ear anyone could hope for and had a sense of what was needed; this was a

CHAPTER EIGHT: David, Our Beloved

tremendous blessing. He had balloons, presents and an ice cream cake. The last thing David tasted was a small nibble of his birthday cake. He tried some just to make me happy.

A most amazing thing happened, after I noticed a young lady catch a glimpse of us all. I thought nothing of it at first, until the next day when she handed me a special letter. She peeked into our room and said, "I never have done this before; written a note to a stranger, but I felt it would be unfair to you to not share what I have learned through God about your son!" I thanked her and took the letter. This is what she expressed, "I felt so overwhelmed today when I saw your family celebrate David's birthday. My heart was so heavy with sadness. I too am a mother. I have two sons seventeen years and fourteen years old. I can't imagine….So as I was in the kitchen in the PCU, I just said, 'God! Why?' I was overwhelmed with God's voice in my spirit, it was undeniable."

She went on to say, "David has great authority. He is a born leader. He has the spirit of a warrior. There is a heavenly army of worshippers that David will assist in bringing glory to God with music. Music is an extension of the heart; it gives force to the desires of the heart. God has seen David's heart and the passion that he carries. It is for the blessing of the nations that he is taking this new position! This is his destiny, a worthy position of honor! You will miss him here on earth, but your joy will be great when you reunite. Heaven is a real place; we are all here for a short field trip. Hold on to your faith; seek to love God all the days of your life. Your reward will wash away all your tears!"

I wept and marveled how accurately she had described David even without any prior knowledge of his personality and talents. I knew she had been inspired of God to be able to reiterate most of what we had learned about his future mission from the priesthood blessing my father had given him earlier. She had expressed his future mission in such a profound way and it gave me even deeper understanding. In Acts 10:34 we learn, "God is no respecter of persons."2

I know when we seek truth, no matter what our faith or belief, (she was of another faith than I), God will surely answer our sincere petitions. However, we need to open our hearts and be willing to accept truth when it is presented to us. We will experience a burning within our bosom and peace within our souls when we seek truth sincerely from God. This is how we can say we know something is true. What greater assurance can we ever expect to receive than from God?

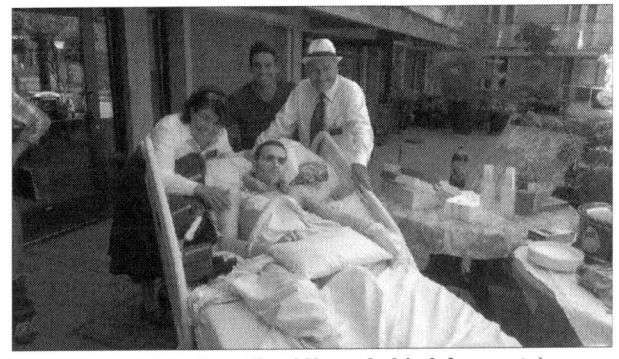

(Easterbrooks at David's early birthday party)

CHAPTER EIGHT: David, Our Beloved

During the party, we took his bed outside, so he could feel the beautiful summer air, which enabled more room for family and friends to visit. He received a few gifts and cards, mainly with our expressions of love for him.

His father wrote the following poem entitled:

"David, Our Beloved"

I think about you everyday
I love you more than words can say.

When I see you suffer it breaks my heart
I dread the reality of living apart.

When I consider the approach of your final sleep
My heart begins to deeply weep.

Thousands esteem you as a wonderful guy
But no one loves you more than I.

You know I have loved you every day
And hope I have shown it in every way.

You are a wonderful example of faith and love
You show what it means to honor our Father above.

You know you are always number one with me
Because you are always tied with the other three.

Life's roller coaster has been both happy and sad
But I have been always grateful to be your dad.

David tried to converse with us, but was worn out due to the shortness of his breathing. Everyone enjoyed having these last precious moments with him before he went under sedation again.

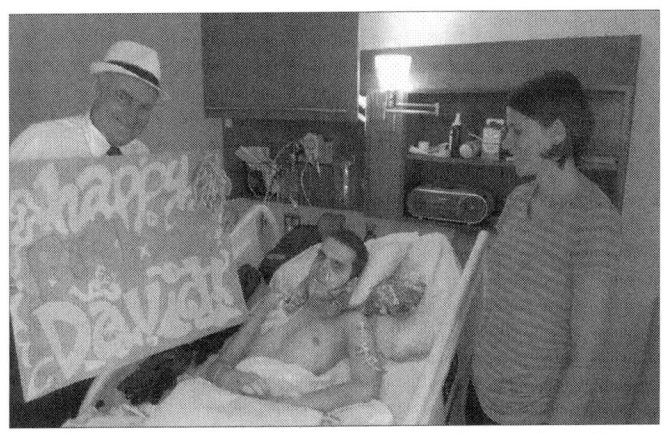

(David with Brother Easterbrook and his sister Laura)

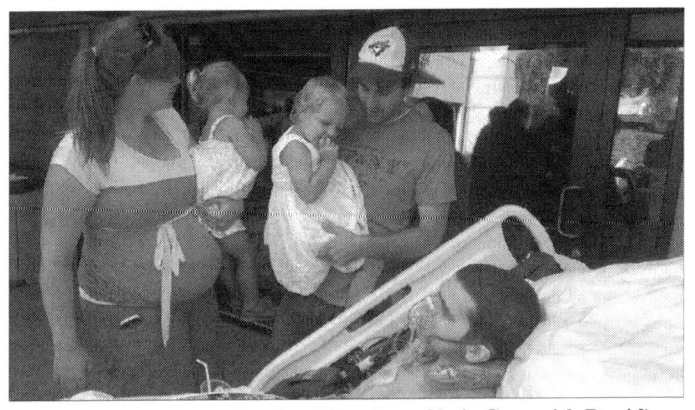

(Laura, Isabelle, Abigail and brother, Chris Gow with David)

CHAPTER NINE: Angels among Us

"Angels speak by the power of the Holy Ghost; wherefore, they speak the words of Christ. 1

The next day was quite difficult for David as he continued to have panic attacks. It became necessary to sedate him continuously. I made it clear to everyone, especially through Face book, that he was under sedation. The family came together to be by his side in the hospital; most everyone was staying nearby. My good friend Leanne Hughes and her husband came to be with us again. The family started sleeping in the hospital and took turns by David's side. I was extremely overwhelmed and exhausted by this time, and really welcomed everyone's support and love. Alana Gow, a cousin of David's father, knew what to do and say, and was also a blessing to have around. We turned on music and movies for David to hear, even though he was under sedation.

I became stressed watching him sometimes partially wake up due to these panic attacks. I decided, with the help of a nurse, that it was necessary to fully sedate him because it was so extremely scary for him to not be able to breathe properly when he woke up, and his neck was hurting tremendously by this time.

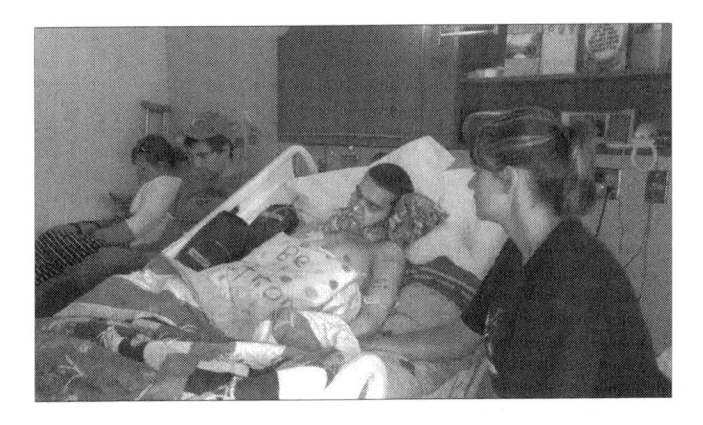

Chris blessed David to peacefully go to his Heavenly Father, but for some reason he fought and hung on. I pleaded to Heavenly Father, begging for his support in helping David relax enough to make the transition into his next life.

I got a distinct impression that the reason he was not letting go was because Kristen was not there with us. I suddenly knew he wanted to give her time to say goodbye. I didn't know if she could make such a trip again, but acted upon the prompting immediately. I felt David guiding me and realized he must be having an "out of body experience" to tell me such a thing. I messaged Kristen to see if she could come that day and told her to not worry about the expense. Kristen was able to get a direct flight, the only seat left on the flight, by that evening. She was a great help and provided such loving support for David. The family gathered that night thinking he might go, but he still hung on longer. I know he wanted to give all of us time still. We all gathered as a family in his room as Kristen and I constantly held his hands; I had one, and she had

CHAPTER NINE: Angels among Us

the other. That night, my daughter Anna suggested we sing. I asked, "What would you like to sing?" She then proceeded with "Love at Home." I got a couple of hymn books out of our car and brought them to his room so we could sing various hymns a cappella style with family and friends. I started the singing of most of the songs as everyone joined in.

On this special evening on July 26th, we all could feel angelic presences very strongly. Even relatives who had never felt such things, commented how wonderful it had been, and believed there had been angels. The palliative nurses mentioned they had never felt such strong angelic presences in a patient's room. They told me they sometimes felt angels just before a patient passed on, but thought the angelic peace they had felt that night was beyond anything they had ever experienced. In the LDS bestseller, Life Everlasting, Duane Crowther provides much insight, "It seems that spirit beings not only summon others through the veil, they also serve as messengers to provide them escort into the spirit world."[2]

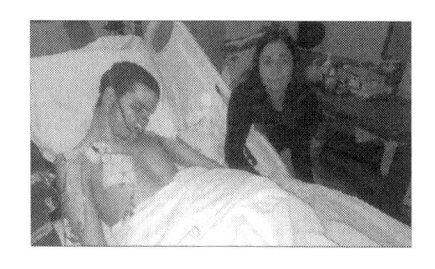

I felt my deceased relatives were among us to take him when he was ready. David tried to wake again and struggled as I put my hand to his forehead many times to settle him down that night. I felt he was again having out of body experiences, but could not gain enough consciousness to tell us about them.

65

Be Still My Soul

David still did not pass away that evening. He was incredibly tough, but we could not let him wake up anymore because he would greatly panic. His neck was also bulging from the cancerous tumor that was still growing. It must have been very painful even with large doses of Methadone.

Kristen put the phone to his ear so many friends could say goodbye the next day. I could feel David listening to these conversations and the talks I had with Kristen and the nurses. It felt like he was standing with us in the room. I could feel his interest and excitement. I also got the distinct impression that David was conversing with angelic presences just before his passing. Later that night, we all decided to watch "Les Miserable" as a family. The room was always warm and peaceful as we felt angels constantly among us. Kristen and I stayed up most of the night taking turns keeping an eye on him. Laura was also in the room that night on July 27th, the last night we had our David with us in mortality.

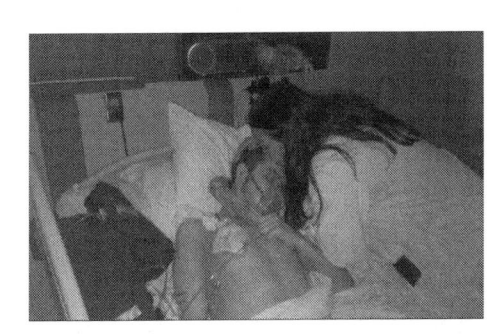

Kristen told me to go to sleep and promised to wake me when it appeared he might be passing. I fell into a deep sleep, deeper than I had been able to for a long time, knowing that Laura and Kristen were there to wake me if necessary. Within

CHAPTER NINE: Angels among Us

three hours, Kristen woke me to tell me he was very close to passing. I felt the overwhelming warmth and peace of angels as I noticed his chest barely rising. Kristen and Laura had fallen asleep, but had woken up just in time. I quickly ran out of the room to get the others, even though I so badly wanted to stay, but I didn't want anyone to miss his passing. My heart was pounding so hard that I thought I might die along with him!

Everyone was sleeping in different places in the hospital, so it took a few minutes to find everyone. A few family members told me they had felt David's spirit give them a hug, and had not been surprised when I told them he was passing. My sister Cate felt his spirit give her a hug goodbye that time at 3:00AM, while she was still gathering pictures of him in Reno. I had somehow missed his hug because I had been in a deep sleep. I felt sad that I had missed the chance to feel his goodbye, but remembered the promise he had made to me about singing in my ear when he got to the other side. I held on to that thought and believed it would happen sometime soon. The Lord had more in store than I had anticipated, but I first had to go through a scary experience!

When I returned back to David's room after waking everyone, he wasn't breathing anymore. I asked Kristen when his last breath had been. She told me I had seen his last breath when I had left the room to get the others. Everyone rushed in after me to say goodbye. Many tears were shed, and then everyone left soon afterwards to mourn. A nurse came in to lay David's body down flat and took the venous port and other insertions out of him. I could not leave the room for some time and spoke to him for a while.

It was especially hard to look at my son's lifeless body in a room that was growing colder by the minute. My deceased relatives, who had been waiting for him, took him away so swiftly that the room had grown cold suddenly. It was quite amazing how frigid we discovered the room to be without their presences. I went into the hallway and thought, "David, where are you"? I didn't get any answer, so I got a little concerned. I then had to face the adversary!

Satan, or one of his spirit messengers, tried hard to get me to disbelieve what I have always known to be true all my life, and how awful an experience at such a vulnerable time! I felt darkness engulf me for a minute when the adversary told me, "See, there is nothing after this life, just look at him now!" I tried to pray vocally, but the adversary tried to bind my tongue, so I kept thinking positively and pleaded for the Lord's help silently. I then immediately heard, "David is busy right now." From all of my readings about near death experiences, I have learned that deceased relatives greet their loved ones and what a joyous celebration it is. Robert Millet and Joseph Fielding McConkie, professors of ancient scripture and authors of many religious texts including, <u>The Life Beyond</u> claim in this book, "For the righteous, the time of death is also a time of

CHAPTER NINE: Angels among Us

reunion, an occasion wherein a person is welcomed once again to the society of loved ones."3 I felt David had been greeted not only by family members, but friends as well. Gabby and Patrick must have been there!

David indeed was busy, and I was grateful of this reassurance through a righteous angelic messenger by the power of the Holy Ghost. We have been told in 2 Nephi 32:3 that "Angels speak by the power of the Holy Ghost." I then felt prompted through the Holy Ghost to go next door to find the lady who had given me the special letter about David a few days earlier. We talked in the hall until I heard a voice call out from her dying sister's room. She ran to her sister's room to soon come out to tell me she had passed away too.

We exchanged hugs and spoke words of comfort and sympathy. I felt especially inspired to tell her more about what she had personally experienced when she had prayed about my son earlier. I then encouraged her to look up the Church of Jesus Christ of Latter-day Saints when she returned home, and explained how it would help her understand the authority the Lord had revealed to her which David possesses, which is "priesthood" authority. The scriptures provide much understanding for us. In Doctrine and Covenants 138:30, it says. "But behold, from among the righteous, he organized his forces and appointed messengers, clothed with power and authority and commissioned them to go forth and carry the light of the gospel to them that were in darkness, even to all the spirits of men; and thus was the gospel preached to the dead."4 I then bore testimony to the fact that the gospel of Jesus Christ has been restored in these Latter-days, since it had been lost for a time on the earth through men's evil distortions, to help us receive personal revelation for our lives; especially in these last days before Christ returns.

After speaking with her, I went back to collect David's belongings and clean the room with Kristen. It was no easy task packing up his clothes and belongings after he had gone. We focused on getting Kristen back home. Everything worked perfectly for her to get back on her booked flight home, just in time. I know the Lord blessed her with this flight; she told me that someone had canceled the last minute enabling her to come just in time. It was again one of those little miracles the Lord bestowed upon us in behalf of David.

It was most comforting to have Kristen with us during this time. She was such a support to David and me especially. After workers from the mortuary took David's body away, we signed some papers and packed up to go to our cabin to mourn. The next day we united as a family to write his eulogy. We thought it best to write it in this manner because it gave each of us a fair contribution, and it really lifted our spirits to reminisce as a family. I asked my son Chris if he would give David's eulogy at the funeral. He collected all our ideas and put together a most inspiring eulogy, which I have included in the next chapter of this book.

CHAPTER TEN: David's Eulogy

"But charity is the pure love of Christ, and it endureth forever; and whoso is found possessed of it at the last day, it shall be well with him."[1]

Good afternoon and thank you for being here today to commemorate the life of David Alexander Gow. As we sat down as a family to discuss what we wanted to say about David, we first turned to what a eulogy means and found it means "to highly commend or praise another." In that light, our family wishes not to brag, but rather commend and praise David in an expression of our deepest love for him and in the best way we know how. We want to do this by telling you of our fondest memories and his strongest characteristics.

David, which means "beloved," Alexander Gow was born on the 7th day of August 1993, weighing in at nine pounds four ounces in the small town of Vanderhoof, BC. From the very beginning, his family spoiled him with affection and loved to make him laugh. He had a laugh that would light up a room. As most of you, if not all of you are aware; David had an inclination towards music from a very early age. Our Mom recounts, "David was a born musician. Even as a baby, he was completely happy in his seat to just listen to me sing as I gave piano and voice lessons. I noticed that he would try to "goo" along and was never restless when music was being performed." "He loved playing on the piano," Mom continues, "even before the age of two, leaning into each phrase as if he was an accomplished musician. His first performance was on stage with me at the age of two. He sang "Michael Row your Boat Ashore" with perfect intonation."

Dad has a very similar recollection. "Shortly after David turned two years of age we purchased an electric piano with a function that was equipped with pre-recorded pieces of classical music. Within hours David was simulating musical performances with the posture, sensitivity and form of a concert pianist. He would pretend to touch the keys lightly for soft tones and then pound them firmly for the louder tones. When the piece would end he would tilt his head from right to left as he quickly retracted his fingers from the keys. He then spread them apart as he raised his hands while his palms faced the piano."

David's disposition as a child showed a streak of independence. Dad recounts a story of when David was no older than two. "One day David, all of a sudden said, 'Hey Dad, I gotta do the dishes.' He then walked over to the dining room table, dragged a chair into the kitchen, climbed up on the chair, placed the drain plug in the drain, turned on the tap, grabbed the detergent bottle, poured the detergent into the pool of sud-generating water, grasped a plastic cup, dipped it into the sudsy water and then proceeded to drink it!"

Anna says, "David's ambitious drive to understand things for himself shone through even as a toddler. As a three

CHAPTER TEN: David's Eulogy

year old, he was a ball of eager energy; he couldn't wait to ride his first bike. He wanted to just get on and go! Trying to be a helpful older sister, I offered to teach him to ride it, but he made that Gow face......pondered for a moment....then replied "That's ok. I can do it." Just half an hour later, he was zipping up and down the road as if he'd always known how!

David was such a sweet child. Anna speaks of a tender moment she had with him when he was very young. She says, "David and 'Love' became synonymous to me the minute he was born. Being born to a family full of avid talkers.... David's grasp of speech came amazingly early. Though I'm not sure of his exact age at the time, he couldn't have been older than two. I remember rocking him in my mother's rocking chair reciting all the names in our family in a sing-song voice as he'd repeat them back. David......David, Laura.......Laura, Anna........Anna, Christopher.......Chris-fa-fer, Ma ma.......Ma ma, Da da........ Da da, then finally I'd say: "I....love....."And his little voice would always answer, "You!"

David's sweetness was something we all remember vividly. Dad says, "David and I would often travel on long-distance trips in the car. On one occasion, when David was six years old we were waiting for the Ferry. He was sitting in the passenger seat and I turned to him and said, "David, do you know how much I love you?" He said, "Oh yeah." (In the tone of voice that implies that there is no secret element to this conversation). I asked, "So how much is that?" He quickly replied, "More than the whole world."

As he began to grow up, this goodness stayed with him. When I was a teenager I loved to get a rise out of people. One evening at a wedding reception I got the idea to get David to do my dirty work. He was only about five at the time. I don't remember what I tried to get him to do, but it was along the lines of saying something to someone that would be upsetting. He stood there with his hands in his pockets contemplating my request. He then looked up at me and said, "No, that's mean. I won't do it." I prodded him, "C'mon David. It's funny." "No," he replied, "that's mean." David's kindness was evident from such a young age of which he carried with him throughout his life. But he also taught me something that day. He taught me the importance of standing firm on true principles no matter who you have to stand up to. It would have been easy for him to waver, especially being so young, but he knew that being kind outweighed the approval of his older brother. Truly this gave meaning to the scripture "out of the mouths of babes" of which David was the messenger that day.

Laura shares an experience she had with him when he was young. "As a very young child, David enjoyed counting and sorting pretend money. This led to his craze for the game of Monopoly. He would ask me relentlessly to play the game over and over again, especially during summer months when we were out of school. I would always agree, even if

CHAPTER TEN: David's Eulogy

reluctantly. As I did not share the same enthusiasm for the game as he did, I would try to speed the game along without him knowing. If he ever left the room for a minute, I'd sneak a few extra five hundred dollar bills into my hand, grab an extra property, or steal some of his money stash. I almost ALWAYS won the game, and he would be baffled at the amount of "skill" I had. He never thought once to question my integrity!"

Staying on this theme of trusting others, David never displayed any fear of strangers. Mom says, "David loved to be around most everyone, no matter what their age and was always looking for a friend. When David was five we came back to the United States and he immediately went looking for friends. One day a neighbor came to me and said, "Is this your son? He is so cute. He just knocked on my door and asked, 'Do you have any kids for me to play with?' One day he even decided that he would buy himself some friends by purchasing candy for the neighborhood to the modest amount of one hundred dollars from his mother's wallet!" He did not fight Mom when he was required to retrieve the unopened candy and money not spent, express apologizes, and serve grounding for stealing. He never stole again!

This same confidence in him shone through as he went door-to-door fundraising. Mom says, "David was quite a salesman, he always got everyone on the block and many blocks over to buy whatever he happened to be selling that week for school fundraising and usually was the top seller.

Before he would leave the house he would announce, "Tonight, I'm going to get ten" and he would. He even went on a walk-a-thon and ended up raising the most money. He was only nine years old."

This confidence led to him developing relationships with some pretty interesting characters. Laura recounts a story of his congenial nature towards those whom he had previously never met. "When David's grandmother, Colleen was recovering from health complications in a rest home, David was intrigued by many of the other patients in the facility. At the age of nine, David went from room to room visiting all of the elderly folks whose mortal lives were coming to a close. Rather than being saddened by their conditions, he used a playful technique to relate to and brighten up the men and women within the nursing home. One day, he stumbled upon a woman whose mind had been clouded by the effects of dementia. Without hesitation or any sense of fear, David befriended the woman and they formulated a humorous bond. She would ask him every so often, "Are you Ronald Reagan's son?" Any time he wasn't around, she'd ask, "Where did Ronald Reagan's son go?"

He would feed her popcorn and play silly games with her. At times she would say slightly aggressive things due to the side-effects of her illness. She would stare at him with pursed lips and say, "Your teeth are real spaced," or "You have a big nose." David saw past the illness and never took offense,

CHAPTER TEN: David's Eulogy

but would simply play along. One time that slight aggression turned into strong aggression telling David she was going to kill him. Without skipping a beat, David just asked "How are you going to kill me?" to which Phoebe pronounced proudly "With a broom!" He found humor in her, where many children his age and older would have displayed fear."

David showed much compassion for others. "David loved to help others in any way he could. We were in awe," said Mom and Rolf, "that he would help babysit twin boy babies whose mother was blind and needed much help; he sought her out himself. He would feed and change and play with them for no pay. He had a way of seeing what others needed and was always willing to help. He couldn't have been older than eleven."

We siblings loved how much our children loved him and how much he truly loved them. When he was in the hospital he would always ask me, "Are the little ones coming?" Our children often would refer to him as "Uncle Dabid." "I was anxious for him to come see my first born in the hospital," Laura says, "because I knew of his appreciation for brand new mortal life. I wanted him to be a large part of my children's lives because David was a large part of mine. He never wanted to put Baby Matty down and David and I had to convince each other to give the baby back to the other."

Anna recounts, "When I think of my little brother, his compassion and gentleness is the first thing I feel. He had this unwavering and natural ability to see a person's heart and understood its intention. His love and concern for his family and friends were always of top priority in all he said and did. One example in particular is when David became a new uncle at the age of eight. You could tell that having such a title so young was something he took special care with. He showed so much concern when little baby Alex would fuss. No matter how often I explained, 'Sometimes babies just fuss,' David would still worry. I finally told him one time, 'You know, when he cries like that, and I know I've done all I can for him, I like to tell myself he's probably got an itch somewhere that he can't scratch.' This eventually put his mind at ease."

I don't think many know this of David, but he really had some great athletic ability. Dad was the one who knows of this best. "As David progressed from toddler to teenager he was always willing to try any athletic activity with me. We would play badminton, play catch with a baseball or a football, hit baseballs at the batting cage in Victoria and Las Vegas, roller blade together in Pocatello, play mini-golf or go bowling in Victoria. He was actually quite talented in all of these sports to the extent of his interest and desire to improve.

David was not particularly competitive. He just enjoyed being successful at building his skill. On one particular occasion he joined me to go ice skating. Prior to stepping on the ice he says, 'I'm not too confident about my ability to skate very well Dad. I am more accustomed to

CHAPTER TEN: David's Eulogy

rollerblading.' I said, 'I get that, but these two skills are pretty similar. You will probably be OK.' When he stepped on the ice he glided around it like a figure skater in training. He could skate forward and backward with equal dexterity and crossover like someone who gives lessons rather than receives them. At this point in time I had been skating for a couple of years and David could skate backwards faster and more smoothly than I could skate forwards. I told him that his style was similar to that of Guy Lafleur!"

Something that I'm sure you are all aware of is that David had a great sense of humor. He would spend hours memorizing and reciting jokes by famous comedians and would tell the jokes so well that one day he was asked for an autograph after performing at his school. David had to inform him that he didn't actually write any of these jokes. David also had the ability to make any movie funnier than it was by constantly commenting at any idiosyncrasies displayed. As I have already said, David loved to joke and laugh.

One of my favorite stories I experienced with David came as we were driving around looking for a certain store in Provo. As we weaved through the streets, I increasingly became frustrated with our lack of success… and it showed. Well, in true little brother fashion, David seized the opportunity to add to my frustration. He began letting out bovine noises from the backseat. He was literally mooing! He would say, "Moooo" then pause and then "Mooooo" again and then let out a little chuckle. After this went on for a couple of minutes, I had definitely had enough. I looked into the rearview mirror and with all the patience I could muster said, "David, I'm really frustrated right now. Can you please stop doing that because it's very distracting?"

You may be thinking, 'Yeah right you said it that nicely?' Well your unbelief right now was matched by David's. "Wow, Chris," he said, "I'm surprised at how calmly you said that to me." This actually made me feel pretty good about myself. So we continued on driving, in peace, desperately trying to find our destination. As typically happens, my phone went off indicating that I had received a text message. I instinctively reached down for it and opened the message. It was from David, it said, "Moo!"

But what really set David apart in this life was his musical talent, especially his singing ability. Mom's side of the family, the Biddulphs and Cooks, had a lot of instrumental and singing talent. But the Gows, the poor Gows, in comparison are a bunch of Heber J. Grants. For those of you unfamiliar with who Heber J. Grant was, he was a prophet of whom another said about his singing ability, "You can practice all you want, just don't do it in my presence!" In any case, David was extraordinary.

I will now read my mother's words about his talents. "David's passion was for singing, even though for many years he dedicated much time to the violin. His step-father Rolf was

CHAPTER TEN: David's Eulogy

very involved in encouraging David to press on with this talent. He played quite smoothly even from the time he first picked it up to the amazement of his brother and sisters and the rest of the family. His hard work and dedication to the violin awarded him usually First or Second Chair status for most performances. He was even asked to perform advanced music in a recital at the University of Las Vegas under the direction of Richard Brunson. David decided to major in orchestra at Las Vegas Academy and again received much recognition for keeping First and Second Chair positions. He enjoyed taking lessons especially with Martha Gronamier in Las Vegas.

David came to Provo to study violin and voice and decided that singing was his greatest passion. He studied under the direction of Darrell Babidge at BYU. David received much recognition from many singing assignments and musicals through Timpview High School and at church. He recorded with Jim Condie on quite a few occasions and put many of his recordings on YouTube with much popularity." (Jim Condie has helped us put together a CD of most of his recordings. These are yours for the taking as a gift from David.) He also performed in Madrigals and A cappella Choir through the direction of Paul Larsen at Timpview High school.

David put others first. This was something that he learned and displayed at a very young age. Our sister Anna has an amazing memory and recently recounted this story about him. "I remember a story of a talk Chris gave in church one year on Mother's Day. Chris spoke of a time when David picked dandelions for mom and after presenting them to her ran back outside announcing 'Now I'll go get some for myself!' Chris then spoke of learning to put others before oneself. I never forgot that."

This selfless, caring disposition was quite apparent when Mom caught him on the phone in a deep discussion to help someone just after he had received the devastating news of his terminal cancer in January. As his condition began to deteriorate, David did not want others to worry so he mostly posted positive things on Face book. Not many really knew how serious his situation was. His dream was to see Celine Dion and he had always been inspired by her music. His dream came true back in March because of Donny Osmond's caring attitude to make this happen. He also wanted to see the Donny and Marie Show and enjoyed it just as much as Celine Dion. He mentioned how enjoyable it had been to go back stage with them and be treated like family!"

Throughout his treatment and subsequent deterioration of his body, David remained positive and upbeat. He did not complain or show anger towards anyone, but continued to love others, show kindness and kept his sense of humor. As Rolf had said to me during David's final days, "He's a hero." This man, David Alexander Gow, was and is such a good man. He is a beloved son, brother, grandson, uncle, cousin and friend to many. The amount of mercy and love he spread to others has

CHAPTER TEN: David's Eulogy

most assuredly been imparted unto him and although the last year of his mortal life came with excruciating challenges, the Lord has received David back home to never suffer that pain again.

In closing I would like to share some words from one of David's favorite hymns entitled:

"Abide with Me Tis Eventide"

>Abide with me; 'tis eventide.
>The day is past and gone;
>The shadows of the evening fall;
>The night is coming on.
>Within my heart a welcome guest,
>Within my home abide.
>O Savior, stay this night with me;
>Behold, 'tis eventide.
>O Savior, stay this night with me;
>Behold, 'tis eventide.
>
>Abide with me; 'tis eventide.
>Thy walk today with me
>Has made my heart within me burn,
>As I communed with thee.
>Thy earnest words have filled my soul
>And kept me near thy side.
>O Savior, stay this night with me;
>Behold, 'tis eventide.
>O Savior, stay this night with me;
>Behold, 'tis eventide. 2

Be Still My Soul

Oh David, sweet, sweet David. We love you. We will miss you, but one day we will abide again together. God bless you and God be with you 'til we meet again.

(Rolf, Helen, David and Cate at David's choir performance)

(Timpview High School "A cappella Choir")

CHAPTER TEN: David's Eulogy

(David's violin solo with choir at Timpview High School)

(One of David's solo performances)

(Getting ready for a theatrical performance with Ben Jacob)

Be Still My Soul

(David with friends, including Amy Smith)

(Family Monopoly time with David)

CHAPTER TEN: David's Eulogy

(Laura, Matty Jr and David at the park)

(Uncle David with Baby Benton Alms and Baby Isabelle Gow)

(Rolf, Helen and David in Provo, Utah)

Be Still My Soul

(David with father, and sisters, Anna, and Laura in Parksville, B.C

(Young David)

(David with Mom, Helen Bertler at high school graduation)

CHAPTER ELEVEN: Let Not Your Heart Be Troubled

"Peace I leave with you, my peace I give unto you, not as the world giveth, I give unto you. Let not your heart be troubled, neither let it be afraid." 1

Since David had lived in four different states in the U.S, three different places in B.C Canada, and had family in the US, and Canada, we decided it was necessary to plan three memorials. We first had a smaller funeral in Victoria, B.C Canada to accommodate his dad's side of the family and our past friends, since his dad and I had grown up in Victoria. David had also come to know many volunteers, nurses and doctors who loved him dearly in Vancouver while he was being treated at B.C Children's Hospital and Canuck Place. It seemed very necessary to have a funeral here with these special people who loved us for so many years. I was very glad to see staff from Canuck place attending this first funeral. Our great friends, Elder and Sister Easterbrook, who were still serving a mission in the area, came to support us as they always had.

I have been heartbroken on quite a few occasions in the past, and thought burying my precious child would be somewhat comparable to these experiences, but instead, I found the Savior's love and comfort bringing me great understanding and peace. I could tell that my children were also being peacefully blessed, which brought even more relief.

Be Still My Soul

I actually felt joy for what David had been called to do on the other side; be a missionary. It is not how I had anticipated his missionary farewell to be, but was glad he had been called and the peacefulness of this reality has remained with me. I can bear testimony to the fact that the Lord will not leave us comfortless, especially when we are obedient and accepting of his will on our behalf.

David's spirit came to me the night before that first funeral, and, yes, he sang in my ear as he had promised! I could clearly understand the passage he brought to my mind and spirit, which were words from one of his recordings "There's a higher window shining down on you tonight," a most awesome experience. David always kept his promises, especially to his mother!

The first funeral took place on August 1, 2013 at 3PM. We had a special viewing and slideshow presentation prior to the memorial, which included his beautiful singing recordings. David had devoted much time to perfecting his natural singing ability and had put together a professional sounding album with the help of Jim Condie, who has a recording studio in Orem, Utah. During this slideshow tribute, there were priceless shots of his life that have been included in this book.

We decided to have a procession, with pall bearers, before his body was taken away to be transported to Utah for another funeral and burial. My son, Chris, gave the eulogy, which everyone found most delightful and inspiring. We then

CHAPTER ELEVEN: Let Not Your Heart Be Troubled

were blessed with a beautiful musical number sung by Melissa Smith, the wife of one of our friends from Victoria. She was accompanied by my past vocal teacher and friend, Susan Young, followed by my daughter Laura's powerful talk and testimony. Laura's testimony can be found in the last chapter of this book.

My daughter Anna expressed her sweet love for David, followed by my testimony. The hardest thing I've ever had to do was to publicly bear my testimony at this time, but I wanted to fulfill David's wishes. I felt strongly, while expressing my testimony, that David was with his cousin Colin, who at the age of twelve, had passed away years prior from leukemia. I had a very strong impression to mention this out loud. Colin's mother, who is David's father's sister, broke down in tears. I think she felt it to be true as well. David's father and his step father, my husband Rolf, also bore powerful testimonies. I know David was pleased because these had been his wishes.

My father, Howard Biddulph, David's grandfather, concluded the memorial service with an inspiring talk about how important it is to "not shrink" when faced with adversity, and how David faced his challenges with such dignity and final acceptance. The message that was conveyed, which was from a past talk given by Elder Bednar, was simply this, "Do you have enough faith to *not* be healed"? My father expressed how this kind of faith is the greatest in the Lord's eyes. My father also shared his testimony including experiences that have

Be Still My Soul

demonstrated David's care and consideration for others. My father gave this talk via Skype from Utah. His testimony has also been included in the last chapter of this book.

We ended with, "Be Still My Soul" because it was the last song from a series of songs we were listening to just before David's passing. These words are most appropriate for what David, our family and his friends had to endure:

Be Still My Soul

Be still, my soul: The Lord is on thy side;
With patience bear thy cross of grief or pain,
Leave to thy God to order and provide;
In every change he faithful will remain,
Be still my soul: Thy best thy heavenly friend
Thru thorny ways leads to a joyful end.

Be still, my soul: Thy God doth undertake
To guide the future as he has the past,
Thy hope, thy confidence let nothing shake;
All now mysterious shall be bright at last,
Be still, my soul; The waves and winds still know
His voice who ruled them while he dwelt below.

Be still, my soul; The hour is hastening on
When we shall be forever with the Lord,
When disappointment, grief, and fear are gone,
Sorrow forgot, love's purest joys restored,
Be still, my soul; when change and tears are past,
All safe and blessed we shall meet at last. 2

CHAPTER ELEVEN: Let Not Your Heart Be Troubled

I hired a violinist to play a medley of David's favorites while people arrived. She also played during the procession of carrying his beautiful casket. He looked just like a missionary, in his suit and tie. We placed his violin, a hymnal, and his scriptures upon the casket.

After the service, we greeted and visited with many friends and family members over light refreshments. A formal viewing of the slideshow was presented at this time. I especially enjoyed visiting with family and friends I had not seen in years, some for nearly twenty-five years. Our good friends the McCues put their vacation plans on hold so they could work in the kitchen to be of loving support for us. They also put us up at their house on many occasions. We went home absolutely exhausted, but most grateful for all our wonderful friends, especially the Hughes and McCues for their willingness to come and be of such tremendous help.

I had a heavy heart again traveling back to Utah along the same path we had taken David only a few weeks previously. All our children came to Utah for this second funeral. When we got there, we were greeted most warmly by neighbors and ward members. My sister Barbara Sorensen came with food and hugs for us all. They stayed in the room across from us on one night, and our daughter Mohna and husband stayed in the same room with their children, scattered throughout the house, on the next. Our other children and their father stayed across the road in another house and were with us in the daytime. Another daughter stayed with friends who lived in the area close by. My good friend, Laura MacDonald stayed with us another night and uplifted me tremendously.

It was a "grand central station" within the walls of our home! Family and friends came from many states including, Nevada, Utah, Virginia, Texas, Idaho, and Illinois, as well as Canada. We were thrilled that so many had been able to come to the Utah funeral, with it being at a difficult time, in the middle of the week and during the summertime. We chose August 7th for his funeral date because it was also his twentieth birthday. The first viewing took place at Walker and Sanderson funeral home the night before. The DVD presentation with his singing, and life pictures were presented during this viewing.

CHAPTER ELEVEN: Let Not Your Heart Be Troubled

The lineup for the morning viewing was quite long. Many had come to pay their respects. Even Debbie and Donny Osmond made it. Donny was still recovering from surgery and came on crutches. I hadn't seen so many family members together in so many years. Over sixty had shown up to be there with us. There were also a number of David's friends who came, including many friends of my own. I broke down in the arms of my dear friend Diane Shapcott. I know it would have been jammed packed if everyone who had desired to come had been able to.

The funeral started with a beautiful viola prelude by my cousin Josh Lohner, the grandson of Clynn Barrus, who is every bit as professional as his grandfather, he sounded absolutely superb. He was accompanied by his fiancée at the time, Emily Warner. They played many of David's favorites as people came to sit down. Each person was given a CD of David's recording "Be Still My Soul" at the door of the chapel. As I mentioned earlier, we were able to put this together just

Be Still My Soul

before his passing.

My son Chris gave the eulogy, and the same testimonies and talks that had been given at the first funeral, were recited once again. When I bore my testimony, I found myself telling his friends that he would have not wanted them to be devastated. My friend Sandy Stevenson told me she had strongly felt David's spirit beside me as I had been speaking. Emily Bean, David's close friend and occasional singing partner, sang "The Prayer" with David's past vocal teacher, Darrell Babidge. Darrell had always been most supportive in helping David accomplish his singing goals. He had worked closely with him for a couple of years through his studio at BYU. We thought the song to be most fitting, especially with it being one of Celine Dion's past hits.

(Ruby Flickin, Kristen Bean, Alyssa Loosli and Emily Bean)

CHAPTER ELEVEN: Let Not Your Heart Be Troubled

My father spoke again of "not shrinking in the face of adversity," and our Bishop, Scott Jacob, gave a beautiful talk on how we will be compensated in the next world for what we lose in this life. This promise reiterated by our first beloved prophet of the Church of Jesus Christ of Latter-day Saints is most comforting, "All your losses will be made up to you in the resurrection, the prophet Joseph Smith declared, provided you continue faithful, by the vision of the almighty I have seen it." 3 Bishop Jacob was most supportive during our entire ordeal. We ended the service with "Be Still My Soul," sung by a few past Madrigal singers, all young ladies, including Kristen, who had sung with David while attending Timpview High School. It was nice to see his choir director Dr. Larsen, and past violin teachers and conductors from Las Vegas attend. I remember how overwhelmingly powerful the song became towards the end. David could be heard by those with spiritual ears. My sister Barbara, and Kristen told me they had heard him clear as day! Immediately following the service, many friends and family members came to the East Lawn Memorial Hills Cemetery for David's burial. Rolf offered the dedicatory prayer on his grave, and Bishop Jacob presided again. Everyone said their goodbyes and many, including myself, hugged the casket.

David was buried next to my dad's sister, Barbara Biddulph, who at the age of five, died due to congestive heart problems. They both have the same birthdays! David was present in spirit again at the burial. Emily Bean came up to me, with tears in her eyes, and told me David wanted me to know that he loved me so much. She said this with such feeling; as if it had come from David's own lips. How greatly comforting this experience had been for me.

I am sure he made his rounds with most everyone, including my mother, who needed his comfort especially. She told me she felt his spirit engulf her! Knowing David, he would have not left anyone out, whether they could feel him or not. After the burial, family and close friends gathered for a beautiful meal that was put on through the Relief Society. My dad suggested that we sing to David, since it was his twentieth birthday. I led the singing.

It was a joyous experience for everyone and lightened everyone's mood. My cousin, Joyce Whitaker told me her autistic daughter, who also has Down's syndrome and is echoletic, was so thrilled and joined in the singing most enthusiastically. Our friends, with the last name of "Morris," have a son who suffers from Down's syndrome as well. He took one look at David during the viewing and confidently told me that David was on his way to the Celestial Kingdom!

CHAPTER ELEVEN: Let Not Your Heart Be Troubled

Corbin, my niece Kerensa's son, who usually is in his own world due to autism, leaned into my father and hugged him for quite some time. We were all blessed tremendously. Pictures were taken by our daughter Mohna Thuernagle, and my sister Cate Vail.

(Josh Thuernagle at David's casket)

(Mohna and family from right: Caleb, Jon, Andrew and Josh Thuernagle)

David's father put on another memorial in Vanderhoof. I heard that it had been a great success. Many had turned out to pay their respects. I had promised to help my daughter-in-law Laura with the twins, with her being so close to delivering their third daughter, so I was not able to attend. I was glad the memorial had been well attended there.

CHAPTER TWELVE: Ministering of Angels

"...There are no angels who minister to this earth but those who do belong or have belonged to it."[1]

I felt quite exhausted after everyone left, but the same peaceful feeling that had been carrying me for months did not disappear due to the mercy of the Lord. We traveled back to Canada shortly after the funeral for we had a new granddaughter soon to arrive. When we finally arrived to our cabin in Nanaimo, I had a heavy heart missing David, but after reflecting upon my experiences, I realized just how much help, even from the other side we had received. This brought peace, even at such a difficult time.

I had especially felt my Grandmother Ruth Biddulph's support, which helped me know which things to be concerned about, "when," as well as "what" to do next. Her spiritual promptings had been such a great blessing. I know our loved ones who have passed on, come at important times to inspire bless and assist us. President Joseph F. Smith has claimed, "In like manner our fathers, and mothers, brothers and sisters and friends who have passed away from this earth, having been faithful and worthy to enjoy these rights and privileges may have a mission given to them to visit their relatives and friends upon the earth again, bringing from the divine Presence messages of love, of warning, or reproof and instruction, to whom they have learned to love in the flesh."[2]

Be Still My Soul

I am still amazed how much I felt her influence. Soon after David's passing, we immediately had to plan two funerals, get things prepared for his burial, transport his body to Utah and get our traveling plans underway just within a few days. I recall the cabin being extremely warm because of angelic presences. It felt as if my grandmother had been standing next to me telling me what to remember to do or check on next. I've had a few experiences with angels to my recollection throughout my lifetime, but these experiences have increased so much in number and intensity since David's passing.

The gift of the "ministering of angels" is mentioned in my patriarchal blessing as one of my spiritual gifts from the Lord. I do have other gifts, but the Lord has especially blessed me with this gift. We all have been given gifts of the spirit to help us through the challenges we will face in this lifetime. I do believe, though, that we need to live righteously, and love more fully to be able to exercise their greatest power and influence in our lives. I was told that "angels would abide with me" and would be there to "prompt me in the important decisions I should make." I received this blessing from my Grandfather Lowell Biddulph when I was a teenager. He has been one of those angels in the past and now with my grandmother presently, who have been prompting me "in the important decisions I should be making." I've had impressions that they are helping David prepare more fully for the mission

CHAPTER TWELVE: Ministering of Angels

the Lord has called him to perform in the Spirit World. I also know David comes to comfort and bless us here as well.

When we sense promptings and whisperings of a spiritual nature, they often come from our deceased family members. In the book, The Message, Lance Richardson is greeted by past friends and deceased relatives during his near death experience. He was told by messengers from the other side, "In most cases, Lance, when you pray to God for help, it is your dead relatives and loved ones who are sent by God to help you in answers to your prayers."[3] He makes this conclusion, "I have never understood nor thought of how God delivers assistance to us. With billions of children, what more perfect plan could he use than through righteous family members? It made me think about how often I may have been given inspiration from God through ministering family servants of God. ...once again I felt that burning warmth inside, testifying to me that it was."[4] The know the love of God is so tremendous that it makes sense that he sends our deceased relatives, who love us the most, to act as ministering angels to comfort and protect us.

Not everyone can detect and feel angelic presences and promptings, but I know our ability to feel and hear can greatly be enhanced when the Lord allows or deems it necessary through His great love for us. Consider this passage by Millet and McConkie, "Between us and those in the spirit world a veil has been drawn, yet it is not impenetrable...by permission of the Lord, persons on either side of the veil may be manifest to those on the other, but this is by law and according to the order which God has established."[5] I know if we pray for God's help, the Lord will surely send it.

My ability to feel and hear, although I have never seen angels, has increased greatly since David's passing. I believe spirits may linger for some time after they leave their bodies, and then come and go depending upon their missions and assignments given through the Lord. Actually, I think they may be with us more than we realize. I believe we can be blessed to feel them, especially when we are in need of help in some way, and especially if we pray for God's help and influence. I also believe through increased righteousness on our own part, especially when we serve each other, we will become more aware they are with us.

Since David's passing, I have tried to live more righteously by praying and reading the scriptures often, and have tried to become more aware of my thoughts, words and actions. Joseph Smith, our first beloved prophet of the Church of Jesus Christ of Latter-day Saints, has so beautifully stated, "If we live up to our privileges the angels cannot be restrained from being our associates."[6] I desire to have angels as my close associates and want my family now, more than ever, to be pleased with my efforts in trying to live more righteously. Living righteously doesn't mean we are perfect, it means we are striving to become perfected.

CHAPTER TWELVE: Ministering of Angels

Donald W. Parry, professor of the Hebrew Bible at BYU, and author or coauthor of over thirty books and numerous articles on the Bible, quotes President Joseph F. Smith in his latest book called Angels, Agents of Light, Love and Power saying, "I believe we move and have our being in the presence of heavenly messengers and heavenly beings. We are not separated from them... I claim that we live in their presence, they see us, they are solicitous for our welfare, they love us now more than ever." 7 I truly have experienced this and have felt David's love even stronger as time has passed. A feeling of peace has remained with me. When I get sad or frustrated, I have sensed David's comforting spirit and help.

I know David has prompted me to do certain things at important times. At the funeral, I felt him prompt me to invite certain friends to our family reception and luncheon. I thought I felt his loving hand on my arm while we were awaiting the arrival of our latest granddaughter Olivia. He actually suggested the name before his passing. It felt exactly how he always had lightly touched my arm when he wanted to get my attention to show his love for me.

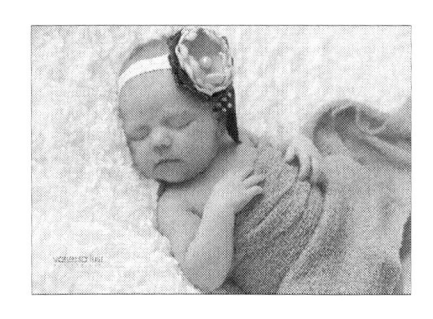

Just before Olivia's arrival, I sensed angels in Isabelle and Abigail's bedroom. My granddaughters pointed and smiled at things I could not see with my own eyes! I believe

105

the veil is very thin, especially for little children, due to their innocence and purity. My sister Barbara mentioned how her granddaughter Harley Sue had smiled and played with someone, no one else could see, at David's burial. Since David loves babies so much, we thought it just had to have been him! We have learned we have another grandchild on the way. My daughter Anna and her husband Ryan, who have been trying for quite some time to have a baby, are expecting now; another great blessing from the Lord.

Another time I've felt David's presence was when we were traveling back to Provo after a visit with Mohna and her family in Idaho. While crying and listening to David's CD, I suddenly felt prompted to give one of his CD's to Celine Dion. I felt a calmness come upon me. It was as if my David had dried my tears. I texted Debbie Osmond about the possibility of having them give the CD to Celine and found out that they had missed getting David's CD at the funeral somehow. I had assumed they had got one and was very glad he had prompted me to ask if they had. I soon found out that Donny had given one to Celine; I know David was pleased!

I also was prompted to give out David's CD at church through the Relief Society, at his past high school through the choir teacher Dr. Larsen, and again publicly through Face book to those who had not been able to go to his funeral. We gave away copies at Canuck Place, B.C Children's Hospital and at the palliative unit in the Nanaimo Hospital in Canada as well.

CHAPTER TWELVE: Ministering of Angels

It had been quite a treat to meet up with past nurses and staff members from these places. We were greeted so warmly and lovingly. It was a blessing to visit and see most of the nurses who had worked with David, on the same shift, the day we felt inspired to drop off flowers and CD's. We ended up giving away almost all of the six hundred copies of David's CD that I had ordered through Jim Condie in less than four months.

I have been able to feel David's presence on many other occasions as well. When my husband and I celebrated our twelfth anniversary after going back to Canada shortly after his funeral, we felt it to be of no coincidence that "You Raise Me Up" was suddenly played loudly between the quiet background music at this Greek restaurant! Rolf and I felt the spirit strongly and started crying, knowing that David had been with us. Also on one evening at home, I thought I sensed his beautiful singing voice in harmony with me as I played and sang "Abide with Me Tis' Eventide." I could also feel many other presences, as if a small choir had joined in. The Holy Ghost warmly engulfed me to verify that this had been so.

I had a most unusual experience when I had to learn a fancy arrangement of "I am a Child of God" for an upcoming primary program. I've always disliked playing with both hands in the treble clef, especially when there are many ledger notes, but was able to confidently learn the piece, even though it was beyond my comfort zone. I had asked Heavenly Father for help and had prayed diligently. It was awesome to have

Be Still My Soul

Heavenly Father send my very own son to help me. I was sure that it had been David by the manner in which he prompted me. We had practiced music together on so many occasions and I recognized his style and mannerisms.

I was able to perform the song beautifully, even though I was nervous when it came time to perform it publicly. My hands somehow, stayed on the proper notes with much expression, even though I was shaking like a victim of Parkinson's disease! Usually if I get nervous when playing in public, I hit wrong notes or play timidly, but not on this occasion. I suspected my David had something to do with this. The Lord blessed me due to my willingness to work hard and trust in his ministering help.

My sister Barbara also felt David's presence and help while she worked on a harmony she decided to make up for "You Raise Me Up." She was given the opportunity to sing this very song at her school, and wanted to sing along with David's CD. She was concerned about how an improvised harmony to his CD might turn out, and prayed earnestly about it. She told me she felt David had inspired her with the harmony and was with her in spirit as she sang. It was so moving for all, that she, or rather I should say, "They" received a standing ovation!

I have especially felt David's spirit when engrossed in the scriptures, while teaching school, visiting my parents, singing and playing the piano, listening to spiritual music, or in

CHAPTER TWELVE: Ministering of Angels

the process of writing this book. I know he is near and watching over us. Many friends have recalled experiences where David has come to comfort and bless them. I invited some of his friends, including Kristen, to his grave site soon after his passing.

(David's gravesite at East Lawn Memorial Cemetery)

One of his friends, Emily Adair, told me she had an experience where she actually heard his voice give her a blessing of comfort. This makes sense to me because David holds the priesthood, and if there was no one else to give her a blessing at that time, why not her dear friend David? Millet and McConkie have expressed, "We share with our fellow servants on the other side of the veil...the same gospel, the same priesthood, the same responsibility to act under the direction of the keys of the priesthood, and the same right to the Holy Ghost by which we are to teach, preach, and bless others."[8] I know David is continuing his same priesthood duties from beyond the veil.

Kristen also shared a time when David had come to her

when she was extremely sad and missing him. He comforted her in such a manner that enabled her to finally go to sleep after so many days of not being able to. She told me he has been with her especially when she decided to make changes in her life to come back to the Church of Jesus Christ of Latter-day Saints. David is most definitely ecstatic about this. She calls him her missionary. Kristen's powerful testimony can be found in the last chapter of this book.

On September 15, 2013 I asked my father for another priesthood blessing for comfort. I felt the Holy Ghost descend upon me, causing me to burn all over. The Lord first mentioned how He was pleased with my pursuit in developing my talents more fully in music, writing and teaching. It was especially nice to hear how pleased the Lord was with my acceptance of his will for David and my efforts in helping him prepare for his new life and future mission on the other side.

The Lord told me, "You were foreordained to be David's mother," and revealed that I had known all my children in the pre-mortal existence before we came to this earth. David and I, as spirits in the pre-existence, shared our love for music together. We had a close bond there as we did here in this life. The Lord also counseled me that he wanted me to continue to gain closer bonds with my children, grandchildren and siblings, so I can help them more fully in their lives. When we serve each other here on earth, we are acting as earthly ministering angels.

CHAPTER TWELVE: Ministering of Angels

I believe David has been given the opportunity to act as one of the Lord's ministering angels here on this earth, and will also preach the gospel as a missionary in the spirit world because of his pure unconditional love for others. I also know he will use his musical talents there to bless and inspire all he meets. Brent L. Top, who is a professor and Chair of Church History and Doctrine for BYU and who has studied and written about the near death experiences of religious and nonreligious people for decades quotes Neil A. Maxwell in his book, <u>What's On the Other Side</u>? Maxwell is a former apostle for the Church of Jesus Christ of Latter-day Saints, who has since passed on to the other side. Maxwell claimed during his lifetime, "On the other side of the veil, there are perhaps seventy billion people. They need the same gospel, and releases occur here to aid the Lord's work there. Each release of a righteous individual from this life is a call to new labor's...though we miss the departed righteous so much here; hundreds may feel their touch there." 9 It had been revealed to me early that David had an important calling on the other side and I have accepted and understood this from the beginning. I know he will work in the spirit world with other priesthood holders, including his own deceased family members, to preach the gospel to those who are willing to listen.

Through this priesthood blessing, I was also promised that my life would be prolonged. This was quite sobering because three days later my husband and I got in a car accident, that wasn't our fault, which could have taken our lives if it had not been for the protection of guardian angels. Instead of having a head on collision with the car that headed straight for us, we hit in such a way that caused the other car to flip into the air over top of us, just missing us. Unfortunately our car was totaled from the impact, but we walked away without a scratch! The teenager who hit us, ended up with only minor injuries, even though she had landed upside down.

We know our protection was not a coincidence. If the Lord has work for us to do here in mortality, he will preserve us. I know this for a surety. This has been made clear through Duane Crowther in, <u>Life Everlasting</u>, when he claims, "There is evidence that some mortal beings are watched over and shielded from danger by spirit-world beings functioning as guardian angels. Peter Johnson, as he went into the spirit world was met by a spirit being who said, "You did not know that I was here." Peter replied, "Who are you?" The reply: "I am your guardian angel; I have been following you constantly while on earth."[10] As I reflect back, I know I have felt the influence of guardian angels throughout my lifetime.

God has plans for us that are beyond our scope of understanding sometimes, but I have faith that his hopes and dreams for us are far better than anything we could ever imagine, plan or hope for. I can testify to the fact that we can find answers to whatever is troubling us, or not making sense in this life with our limited perspectives. I know if God needs

CHAPTER TWELVE: Ministering of Angels

us on the other side, we will come to understand this as I know David has. "There is a reason for everything," as David always put it so simply. David had faith in the Lord's will, even though it did not match up with his own hopes and dreams while he was still here in mortality. I feel David understands his mission more fully now, and is very happy about it and the choices he will be able to make, as promised in the blessing my father gave him.

I was also counseled to regularly reach out to my mother, who needs my love so desperately. Unfortunately, she can't walk, and has lost most of her eyesight due to a stroke because of a botched surgery. Her needs are incredibly great. One day as I was busily going about my work, I had the distinct prompting to go check on her. My parents live in a care facility just down the street from us. At first I ignored the prompting because I was in the middle of learning music and don't like leaving my practicing, especially when I get so enthralled with it. The prompting came again, "Leave now and go be with your mother!" I even got a bit of a chastisement for not doing it right away, so I put my music down and went.

When I got to my mother, she was close to crying because of the awkward position she had somehow got herself into. She told me she had been praying for me to come. I put her in more comfortable position and spent time visiting and uplifting her. My husband had taken my dad to the doctor leaving her by herself for awhile. They knew she would be taken care of if she pushed her button, but she just wanted me, knowing I was home that day. I was glad I had listened!

How many times do we feel promptings and don't act upon them? God sends us angels to guide us "...in the decisions we should make." A very important prompting I received a few months after David's passing was to go to the temple at a most crucial time. I had lost contact with a dear friend and was sad she had not contacted me during the time of David's death. I was having a tough time wondering why she had not shared her love and concern at such a difficult time for me. Deep down I knew there had to be a reason because it wasn't like her to not say anything, but I have always been afraid of rejection.

On this particular day, I felt a very strong impression to go to the Provo temple in the afternoon. Rolf and I usually go in the evenings. Upon entering the chapel of the temple, there was my friend. She is an ordinance worker and at this particular time was greeting everyone outside of the chapel. She was so happy to see me and said we should catch up. I was perplexed why she hadn't said anything about not contacting me for so many months. She acted like she hadn't known David had passed away.

I knew I had to contact her to find out what had happened. To my surprise, she hadn't received an important text message where I had invited her to visit David on the last few days he was in Provo shortly before his passing. She

CHAPTER TWELVE: Ministering of Angels

thought I was still in Canada and was waiting to hear from me. I could have lost a very important friend if I had not listened to those sensitive promptings. When we get caught up in ourselves, we miss opportunities for love and service, and even possibly could lose some of our friendships. I am so very grateful to have my dear friend, Debby Rittel back in my life!

It has been wonderful to know the Lord was pleased with my care of David. What a joyous experience to receive such a blessing. I know what things I should to be focusing on now. God gives us the experiences that are best suited to help in our progression of becoming more like Him. This is the whole purpose of our existence, to become more righteous every day until God perfects us someday. I am also grateful to know who I am; a child of God. God wants us to keep progressing towards becoming more like our Savior every day. This is one reason he sent Jesus Christ to the earth as our example to follow. The things we experience and are tested with in this life are but stepping stones to this goal. I am thankful for the blessings of the priesthood in my life that will enable me to truly reach this goal.

It takes faith to believe, and sometimes even more faith to act, but I know as we exert ourselves to loving each other more perfectly, the Lord will bless us more fully. We are loved by the Lord, no matter what we choose to do in this life, but the greatest rewards in the end will be given to those who choose to love and serve him. David truly was an example of charity.

It was so evident in his actions. He put other's needs before his own. He was always kind and did not want to hurt anyone. If he knew his actions somehow hurt someone, he tried to change or apologize for them. He was never puffed up. He did not even realize how incredibly talented he was. He desired constructive criticism and was quite a perfectionist; always working hard to improve.

David bore testimony of the truthfulness of the gospel to many, and associated with everyone, even if they had differing views from his own. David was a friend to everyone; he had no enemies. I've had many people throughout his lifetime say, "Oh, I just love your son!" Most everyone who knew him well would tell me, "David is wise beyond his years." My mother recalls this writing experience with David.

"David lived with us for some time, and knew I was writing a book. I told David I had a job for him. He was interested and began to ask questions. I said, 'Let's set up a desk here on the bed so you can help me. Please, first help me by listening as I talk. Does that sound alright, David?' He said, 'Yes,' so I proceeded with setting up a desk. Our writing began from there. I said, 'David do you know what a bully is?' He retorted, 'I think it is someone who delights in badgering and sometimes even hurting others?' I replied, 'Well, this really happened to me, and I'd like you to listen and give me suggestions about how the writing of this could be improved.

When I was in the seventh grade and even sometime

CHAPTER TWELVE: Ministering of Angels

earlier, I was bullied by a big, mean fat girl. For reasons beyond my control, she hated me. I've reflected upon these bullying experiences and have come to this conclusion; she simply was jealous. I was slim, smart in school, and even good looking, so I was told. Here's something noteworthy that happened. One day, when our teacher was out of the classroom for a time, I will not mention her name; this mean girl suddenly came up from behind me and snatched my purse from my desk. She then began to call on other students to catch the contents!

The worse thing about the whole experience was that she found it amusing to flash my feminine pads publicly!' David's eyes got real big as he said, 'my word, what did you do then?' 'I was sad and wanted to cry.' David interjected, 'But what did you do, I mean, back to her?' 'Nothing really,' I replied. 'This bully wanted me to cry.' David asked, 'Well, didn't you at least yell at her? Or demand the purse back? 'No David, I didn't, but I did want to sock her in the head. I didn't, though. I knew if it came to physical fighting I would surely lose. She was a huge girl and mean as anyone could imagine'

My pads went whirling back and forth as kids so unsympathetically laughed at me. I was totally crushed, and outraged at the same time. It took awhile for me to calm down. When I finally did, I asked for my purse to be returned. David offered this suggestion, 'Couldn't you have gone to another female teacher for help?' I thought, 'Man, that David is a smart young man. He even has great insight into solving life's problems!' I had only anticipated David's suggestions with sentence structure, not in sensible solutions. David was extremely talented in helping others reflect upon and analyze their own problems in a deeper manner. How many teenagers can offer sound advice to their grandparents?"

On many occasions as we spoke mother to son, I felt as if I was talking to an adult with an advanced understanding of love and life. When someone acted unreasonably, he would come up with the many reasons why they may have acted the way they did. David knew how to love imperfect people perfectly. He could not get himself to talk harshly about anyone. David tried hard, in spite of his own personal challenges, to live the gospel, and when he fell short; he always repented and ended up doing the right thing. I am so immensely blessed to have such a special son, and the knowledge that we will be together again someday. His unconditional love has been a blessing to help bring our family closer together. We are forever grateful for you our "beloved" David for seeing each of us so lovingly through your beautiful eyes of understanding.

CHAPTER TWELVE: Ministering of Angels

(David listening to music at home)

(David with Grandma Colleen Biddulph)

Be Still My Soul

(Uncle David with baby Matty) 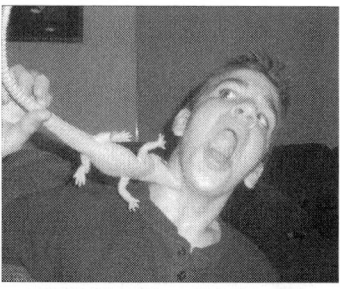   (David at Rosalie's house)

(David with Rosalie Spears)

(David with Caldwell's at Canuck Place)

CHAPTER TWELVE: Ministering of Angels

(David with Emily Bean and friends at Mike Poret's house)

(Prom time)

(David with Emily Adair)

Be Still My Soul

(David and Kristen were inseparable)

CHAPTER TWELVE: Ministering of Angels

(David with Sister Laura at Anna's wedding)

(David and Kristen on a Vegas trip)

Be Still My Soul

(Young David and Sister Anna)    (David with sister Anna)

(David in Missouri on zip line)    (David at friend's house)

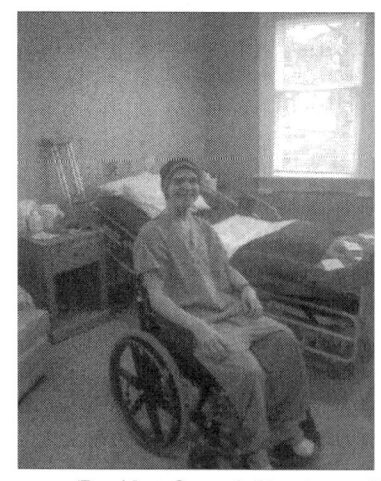

(David at Canuck Place)    (Uncle David with Alex and Laura)

CHAPTER TWELVE: Ministering of Angels

(David with Cousin Taylor Vail)

(Young David on the violin)

CHAPTER THIRTEEN: Family Testimonies

"And by the power of the Holy Ghost, you may know the truth of all things."1

(Testimony of Howard L. Biddulph)

"Do you have enough faith to not be healed?" This question was asked by Elder Bednar of the Quorum of the Twelve in a BYU devotional entitled "That We May Not Shrink. He well observed that it requires great faith to be healed, but emphasized that it requires even greater faith to submit ourselves fully to the will of the Lord. In Luke 42:22, our Savior so perfectly modeled this kind of submission to His Father when he said, "Father if thou be willing, remove this cup from me, nevertheless not my will, but thine, be done." King Benjamin declared in Mosiah 3:19, "For the natural man is an enemy to God ...unless he yields to the enticings of the Holy Spirit, and putteth off the natural man and becometh as a child, submissive, meek, humble, patient, full of love, willing to submit to all things which the Lord seeth fit to inflict upon him, even as a child doth submit to his father."

According to King Benjamin, a true Saint is one who learns to submit his or her will to the will of the Father. Elder Neil A. Maxwell has so eloquently emphasized this when he said, "When we express our desires out of an imperfect perception, and upon learning the Father's desires, we yield to His perspectives and purposes. It is the only surrender that is also a victory!"2

When I heard the shocking news of David's cancer, I immediately received the witness from the Lord that he would not recover. The Lord told me he was being called to the other side. Many in the family, including David, naturally hoped and were determined to exert their faith that he might be healed. I received knowledge through the Spirit that David was to prepare himself for service to the Lord beyond the veil. I watched this conviction grow in David as he gradually submitted his own will to the will he recognized the Lord had for him. I felt it my role to help his mother fulfill her role, which was to prepare him for that mission. This entire book about David shows the glorious way in how she succeeded in helping him make preparation for his passing.

I recall our last conversation together, just before David's final departure to go back to Canada, when we discussed his Patriarchal blessing. I could see that he had accepted the promises made to him through the Patriarch, especially those relating to his preaching of the gospel. It was very evident he had become as the submissive child spoke of by King Benjamin. The very last moment we looked at each other, without verbal communication, for words did not need to be spoken, he looked at me and I looked at him and it was understood that this was goodbye for this lifetime. I felt he understood my thoughts, which were, "Goodbye my beloved grandson David, until we meet again on the other side".

CHAPTER THIRTEEN: Family Testimonies

I bear testimony to the reality of the plan of salvation the Lord has established for us. Through the missions the Lord has in store for us beyond the veil, I know His great work of salvation is being carried forth in the same manner as it is here on earth. I testify to the fact that I have met and encountered real visitations from the other side, including ones from our beloved David. In the name of Jesus Christ, Amen.

Be Still My Soul

(Testimony of Chris Gow)

This morning just after 3:00AM, our beloved David passed across the veil. It is a time of great mourning. He was taken by a vicious cancer (angiosarcoma) that eventually suffocated him. He died peacefully in the Nanaimo hospital as the drugs he was given prevented him from experiencing this pain. That poor boy suffered for over a year with the physical pains of cancer. I feel so sad and can't believe that this has happened. He fell just short of his twentieth birthday. Oh how my heart is wrenched. I feel such pain and loss. I can only imagine what my parents feel. Losing a child would be the hardest thing for me to endure.

As I ponder about life I think about how we are instructed that this life is a test, and I agree. This life is a test but not in the typical way we look at tests. We often see tests and trials as something we need to just get through. As Elder Eyring so humorously put it, "...gripping the arms of a dentist chair while someone pulls out one of my teeth." Yet this is not so. There is enduring and there is enduring well. Enduring our trials well is more akin to what elder Neil A. Maxwell explained as "partaking of life's bitter cup, but without becoming bitter." This is, however, more than just taking it on the chin and smiling in the end. These trials are designed to test our resolve to do the Lord's will no matter how difficult.

Our Heavenly Father lives by a set of laws. These laws govern the universe and they are unalterable. Our ultimate

CHAPTER THIRTEEN: Family Testimonies

goal of reaching the Celestial Kingdom is more than dwelling with God, it means to *be* as God *is*; the Creator of worlds without end. For us to be how He is, where worlds and souls hang in the balance, we must be steadfast in eternal truth and not shrink no matter how hard or how wrenching or how disappointing. Jesus gave His life so we may live again. His agony was so exquisite that it caused Him to bleed at every pore which pain must have been excruciating for His Father to behold. We must be able to be trusted to behold such suffering without intervening with the power that eventually will be bestowed on us, for such things are necessary to the salvation of man.

David learned to have the faith to not be healed and accepted the will of Heavenly Father. He was promised in a blessing from Grandpa that he would not suffer, that many are cheering for him on both sides of the veil, that his passing would be a beautiful experience, and that he would pass peacefully.

The night leading up to David's departure from mortal life saw his loving family sitting by his bedside singing the hymns of the restoration. We sang about family, about the Savior and about the Plan of Redemption. A peace and assurance of life after death enveloped his room so palpable that the nurses exclaimed, "There is a real energy here!" And so it was. The Holy Ghost testified to us and to them of a life after this. It testified of a loving Heavenly Father of whom we all once knew and once dwelt in His presence. We invited the Holy Ghost through "prayers of the righteous" and He imparted a portion of His spirit to comfort us during our greatest time of need.

It is my testimony that God the Father lives. *I know He lives*! I know that His son, Jesus Christ, paid the price for the suffering and agony and despair that we all experienced as David's life slipped away. I know that because of the atonement that all things that seem unfair, such as the passing of a young man before his twentieth birthday, will be made up to us far more than we can comprehend. I know that these truths and many others were restored to the Earth through the Prophet Joseph Smith. The appearance of Heavenly Father and Jesus Christ unlocked the Heavens to this knowledge once lost for centuries. I know that I will see my little brother again. I know that he and I and all the human family will one day be resurrected. We will kneel in awe and reverence before our Savior and bathe His feet in our tears for He made it possible for us to be reunited. I bear this solemn testimony in the name of Jesus Christ. Amen.

CHAPTER THIRTEEN: Family Testimonies

(Testimony of Laura Gow)

There are certain laws and boundaries that govern the incidents of this Earth. While the omnipotent power, which we respectfully call Heavenly Father, is able to alter those laws at times and produce miracles beyond our mortal understanding, in this particular instance, Heavenly Father chose to allow the Earth's laws to govern the outcome of David Alexander Gow's life. In July 2012, David began having consistent pain in his left hip. In December, 2012 he was seen in the emergency room in Nanaimo, British Columbia, Canada where an X-ray showed a large destructive lesion of the left side of his pelvis. He was transferred to Vancouver General Hospital where further investigations showed a large primary destructive lesion in the left hemi pelvis extending into the femur, and a smaller lesion in the right iliac bone. There were also extensive bony metastases involving the right parietal skull, the C5 vertebral body, and other vertebral lesions including C6 and T1. David also had multiple pulmonary metastases. The primary tumor was biopsied and shown to be angiosarcoma.

While no one on this Earth could fathom how such a destructive and terrifying diagnosis was even possible; reality was, that David's life would be considerably shorter than any of us expected. We all imagined David's life to be such that he would first, prepare for and serve a two year mission for the purpose of spreading the Good Word. Second, he would come home, get discovered by a record company, and live a long happy life full of singing and joy. Third, he would be married for Time and All Eternity in the Temple of the Most High.

As his older sister, I was completely, utterly, and totally confused by the fact that he would not be allowed more time on this Earth to fulfill these goals. I questioned everything that thus far I knew to be true. I was totally clouded by my own idea of what life even means. Up until that point, I thought of life as having a body and a spirit combined together. While this mortal life IS a very important step in our eternal progression, I had to do some intense pondering to come to an understanding of what life ACTUALLY is. David received blessings very recently telling him that he would still serve a mission, and that he would use his music and singing to bring further glory to God. He would continue to make choices that would make him happy. While we as mortal beings have a hard time understanding how that would be possible without a body, yet it is true. David no longer has a body. David doesn't need a mortal body to fulfill all the things that were spoken to him in his Patriarchal Blessing. He can do many of those things in the Spirit World. And any of those things that he cannot do in the Spirit World; he will be able to do after he is resurrected. He may not have a body anymore, but he is still making choices, he is just in a dimension that we cannot see with our eyes. Those who have crossed over the veil can see David. When we cross over the veil, we will be able to see him too. I say these things in statements, not questions, because

CHAPTER THIRTEEN: Family Testimonies

they are facts, not speculations. Anyone who will read, ponder, and ask if these things are true, will come to know that they are. These are not just fantasies of the heart. Fantasies of the heart wouldn't even exist if we did not have eternal spirits. Life would not exist if these things weren't true.

I was in the hospital for David's earthly birth, and I was in the hospital for his earthly death. Although his spirit had no choice but to leave his body on July 28 2013, I know he is in good hands. He is with our ancestors who have passed on before. He is still making everyone laugh with his incredible knack for comedic timing. He is probably still quoting Jim Gaffigan and Mad TV. But best of all, he is still singing and using music to produce spiritual sounds that we cannot hear, but we CAN feel. I speak of David in the present tense because he is not in the past. He is still present, and I am so happy that I know that. I may have lost my little brother's body, but through this experience, I have gained everything. I cannot wait to see him again when my mortal test is over. But until then, I will do my very best to pass on the knowledge that I learned from this experience to all those who would listen. In the name of our Savior, who truly exists and exalts, Jesus Christ, Amen.

Be Still My Soul

(Testimony of Don Gow)

It is actually quite difficult for me to explain how I felt during the illness, decline and demise of my precious son, David. From the moment he was born, I felt a profound affection and compassion for him. I have felt that way about all four of our children. Even though each of them is unique in terms of their talents and aspirations, there is a profound, intangible similarity in their spirits that causes people to recognize that they clearly are siblings to one another.

Throughout his entire life David demonstrated that he was so intelligent and teachable, that he was able to absorb and adopt the strengths of his parents and siblings. He could play music and sing like his mother. He could analyze and debate like his brother. He could exercise humor, compassion and warmth like his sisters. He could develop athletic skill in any sport he turned his attention to with the help of his father. He was the "apple of everyone's eye" and he could do anything he needed to do. He was quite autonomous and did not need to be reminded to do chores or take care of basic responsibilities.

In September of 2012, he began to experience serious pain and discomfort. I was totally dependent upon the diagnosis of the local doctors in Vanderhoof and Prince George to understand David's ailment. The only consolation I had at the time was that I knew David could count on me to comfort and assist him to the best of my ability. He continued to suffer with pain in his left hip and left leg for three months without

CHAPTER THIRTEEN: Family Testimonies

anyone being able to recognize the cause. This was very hard emotionally on David and I, because the only things we knew how to do were to pray, to provide as much comfort as possible, and to seek medical advice from CT scans and MRI scans.

It was not until January 2, 2013 that Dr. Shepherd, in Nanaimo, suggested an x-ray to which I wholeheartedly agreed. Although the x-ray revealed the most ominous results, it was still a relief to David and me because we finally came to understand the cause of his pain. Subsequently, David was transferred to the Vancouver General Hospital to undergo the tests that would reveal the severity of his condition.

It was approximately January 10, 2013 when the team of surgeons and physicians entered the hospital room to tell David and me that he was afflicted with angiosarcoma, a rare cancer of the blood vessels. The tumors were so numerous and embedded in his tissues and blood vessels that surgery was out of the question. When they left the room, David broke down in the most sorrowful sobbing I have ever witnessed. He was devastated that his mortal life would not be able to proceed in the manner that he had imagined and desired. Of course, my heart was crushed with compassion for him. All I could do was hug him and say, "We just have to be optimistic and trust in God." Within an hour, he had come to grips with his condition and during the next seven months I never heard him express any sense of pity for himself. Certainly, he was not constantly bright and cheerful, but he constantly emanated dignity and respect towards everyone with whom he interacted. He demonstrated genuine and profound faith which he had been taught throughout his lifetime.

His suffering and passing rank as the most sorrowful experiences of my life, but I have been able to accept these experiences without bitterness or confusion because I have a testimony of the gospel of Jesus Christ. I received the spiritual witness in May of 1979 and this knowledge has helped me endure many disappointments and frustrations since that time.

As a result of consistent prayer and frequent study of The New Testament, The Old Testament, The Book of Mormon, The Doctrine and Covenants, and The Pearl of Great Price, I have a profound assurance that every member of the human race will eventually be resurrected. Everyone will experience the reunion of their body with their spirit. As a result of this sure witness, I know that I will eventually enjoy the marvelous opportunity to embrace my precious son, David. I sincerely share my testimony with you in the name of Jesus Christ, Amen.

CHAPTER THIRTEEN: Family Testimonies

(Testimony of Mohna Thuernagle)

Birth and death are events that happen often around us. Birth is adored and admired for the miracle that is created. We spend much time cooing over a new baby and are filled with anticipation for the many months that are ahead of that. Yet it is amazing to me how death is something many people fear and don't talk about much, even though it is something we all must face. Yes, we do not have scientific fact for what happens after death, which is probably what causes sadness and fear to be associated with death. But that is the beauty of The Church of Jesus Christ of Latter Day Saints. It has given me knowledge, strength, and most importantly, faith, to handle David's shortened time.

From the moment I was told that David had a serious condition, I had peace in my heart. I was not happy about the pain he would have to go through, but I did not fear or deny that he was to face death soon. But still I did not feel angry or sad because I knew where David was heading and that I will undoubtedly see him again. I have faith in knowing I will see David again, even though I have felt great sadness and a deep sense of loss. How unfair it seemed that David would not be able to experience so many of life's milestones like a mission, marriage, children, etc. Only Heavenly Father knows why that is so, and that's what matters.

He has a plan for David, more wonderful than I could ever picture. I miss David tremendously. He had a sincere way with my boys Andrew, Joshua, and especially Caleb. His patience with them, no matter how much they bugged him, always amazed me ever since he was eight years old, and has been around them. He sincerely enjoyed playing with them. I miss his sense of humor that kept all of us constantly laughing. I miss his beautiful musical talent. It is still hard for me to listen to his CD because I hear his voice and I want to talk with him, but I can't. On the other hand, I feel lucky to have his CD, because I will always have his voice to hear when I want to.

Ultimately, I am so thankful to know that David is in a safe place doing wonderful things. I am anxious to be with him again and share our stories of our experiences while we were apart. He loved to tell stories about his experiences. I'm so thankful his physical struggles are but a memory now and that his spirit is free. May we all look forward to and not fear our futures beyond this life. We will be happily impressed, I'm sure of it. I love you David!

Love your Sister, Mohna Thuernagle

CHAPTER THIRTEEN: Family Testimonies

(Testimony by Rolf Bertler)

In early January of 2013, David called me and said that he had the results from the biopsy taken in the Vancouver Hospital some days earlier. I was tense, to say the least. He proceeded to tell me that he was diagnosed with a very aggressive cancer called angiosarcoma and the doctor had given him six months to two years to live!

Silence

I was both shocked and surprised how calmly David communicated this news to me. I immediately felt the Spirit, which confirmed to me that David spoke the truth.

I don't remember how we ended the phone call, but I do recall very vividly that my own feelings of sadness were overwhelmed by not only feelings of deep sadness for David, but also equally deep sadness for my sweetheart Helen, the mother of David.

My Sweetheart wrote in previous pages how I communicated this news to her at the school where she worked at the time. This news changed our lives in an instant, and this moment in time was burned into both our hearts for eternity.

David, as far as I know, never spoke about his fate in such clear terms ever again. He even told his doctors not to talk about his terminal condition. It was my feeling that he did this mainly to protect his family.

During a visit to Provo, his Grandpa Biddulph gave David a blessing that revealed to him that he was called on a mission to the other side. I believe that this knowledge helped him much to accept his condition and to deal with it in the positive manner that he did. David had to suffer a great deal, more than any young man at his age should ever have to, but he was the one who gave strength to all of us throughout this very difficult journey. He was, and still is, a huge example to his family and to his many friends.

Although David was my stepson, I raised him and loved him as if he was my own flesh and blood. I also know that David went to the other side in good standing with the Lord, which gives me peace and comfort; I know he is at a much better place now. David was blessed with many talents, especially musical and interpersonal ones, and I am sure that he has great opportunities to use them now. I love you and I miss you David, but we shall meet again when Heavenly Father calls me home. In the name of Jesus Christ, Amen.

CHAPTER THIRTEEN: Family Testimonies

(Testimony of Kristen Bean)

Where should I begin? I'll start by saying; this year has probably been the hardest year of my life. I've been pushed nearly to the breaking point! I found myself at rock bottom, and nowhere to turn, or so I thought. I've struggled with the "Mormon" church even before I was a teenager. I am the type of person who has to *test the water* to see if it's really as hot as everyone says. I didn't fully begin my search for "self discovery" until I was about thirteen. I ventured out on my own and started testing everything anyone said about the church and its truthfulness, and I just wasn't buying it. I got mixed up with the wrong type of people and began my downward spiral into nothingness. I was lost, confused, and alone.

Turning to drugs and self harm was an escape to help me forget just how alone I thought I was. In the beginning of the year of 2010, I decided to completely come clean and tell my parents that I didn't believe in the Church and never really had a testimony. This wasn't easy for them to hear, but they accepted it and loved me no less than if I were in the Church. I am blessed with amazing parents. Thankfully, I don't think they ever really knew just how far gone I was. I was indulging in dangerous activities and the number of tattoos and piercings on my skin were growing rapidly. I admit I was out of control. But for some reason, I was still here. There were many times where I should have died and many situations in which I was lucky to get out alive. I didn't realize it then, but it was the Lord protecting me. I was always an excellent student, always able to hold a good job, always able to keep my head held high enough to make it through another day alive. I always just thought it was luck, but luck doesn't come with wings; angels do!

My senior year started just like any other. It consisted of getting good grades and fooling all of my friends and teachers into thinking that everything was okay, and that I had my head on straight. Everything changed in Mr. Larsen's Madrigals class when I met David, the boy who would change my life forever. I didn't know it then, but I did know he was special.

David and I started dating on Halloween of 2010. He didn't see my piercings, or my addictions, or my problems. He saw me! He was the first person who ever truly looked at me and told me that everything would be okay. My wall broke down for the first time in my life and I fell in love with him. He accepted me for who I was and saw "my past" as my past, and "my future," as a story that was yet to be written. He was determined to stick by my side until I was exactly where I needed to be. He truly was a blessing from the Lord. He and I were totally opposite in our beliefs. He was strong in the church; I obviously was not at the time. He was always an example to me and was trying to show me the way to gain true happiness.

CHAPTER THIRTEEN: Family Testimonies

David and I continued our relationship for the next few years. At times it was a bit rocky, but we always made it through. I went back and forth in my feelings about the Church. I saw how much happiness it brought David and I wanted that. Of course, he had his own struggles with things. But he always had a testimony, and I loved and envied that. One thing David always told me was to NEVER stop praying, and to never stop believing in angels and miracles.

When January of 2013 came, I received the phone call that stopped my heart and changed my life. David, my best friend and love of my life, had terminal cancer. At first I was angry, I hated God! God had taken away so many of my friends before and now David? I couldn't even stand the thought of praying to God to ease the pain I felt. I immediately went out to Canada to visit David and told him how angry I was and how hurt and betrayed I felt by our Heavenly Father. David looked me straight in the eye and said, "Don't! Don't go back to who you used to be just because of this bump in the road! Don't lose faith and hope in the good things to come! Don't hate God for this!" He really changed my life by saying this; he possibly even saved it. After that first trip to Canada, I decided to change my life. If I was to change myself, I knew I had to completely turn to my Heavenly Father.

When David and I decided to get married, it was the happiest moment of my life. Although I knew deep down that it probably would not happen because of his condition, I didn't care. I loved him and because of him, I loved the Lord. This has been more than I could ever ask for. My anger dissolved through David's love. David accepted the challenge the Lord placed in front of him with full purpose of heart and never took his eye off his faith.

David was the example I needed in my life and an example to everyone who had come into his life. I do admit I was extremely stubborn. After so many years of being inactive and living a totally opposite lifestyle, it wasn't easy for me to get back into the Church, but David always had faith in me. A few weeks before David's passing, we were talking about the future; about my future. This is when he promised to be my guardian angel. I know he will always be with me. His one big wish for me was that I would find true happiness.

David's passing was the hardest thing I've ever experienced in my life, but also the most eye-opening experience to learn from at the same time. People come into our lives for a reason. David touched me in ways no one else could have. The first Sunday after David's passing, I went to church for the first time in years. I am continuing to go to church every Sunday now and am fully active in the Church. I have started to take the sacrament again and will get my temple recommend in the near future. I plan on being in attendance for David's temple endowment, which will be given to him by proxy through his brother Chris. I know none of this would be possible without David by my side.

CHAPTER THIRTEEN: Family Testimonies

I love the Church, and I love that I can say this. I am so grateful for the Atonement. Without it, I don't know where I'd be today. I know that I have a Savior who died for me and who loves me unconditionally, and it is BECAUSE he loves me, that he gives me trials. I can say now, that I am grateful for the trials that have been given to me. The Lord doesn't put you through anything you can't handle if you will just turn to him. I am a witness of this, and will testify of this for the rest of my life. I am so grateful to have known David and was able to love him, and feel the love he gave me so freely. I know he is okay and is with our Heavenly Father and is watching out for me as my guardian angel.

These experiences have humbled me. They have helped me realize just how precious life truly is. I am grateful for music; it is the language that David and I spoke. I know he is up there singing in the choir right now! I am so blessed to have music in my life. It is our closest connection to Heaven. I am so grateful for my family and friends who have stuck by me through thick and thin and have helped me get to where I am today. There is always more room to grow; no one is perfect. I am thankful for forgiveness and prayer to help us all get where we need to be. I am most thankful also for the daily love I feel from my Father in Heaven and the experiences he gave to me to help me change. I am excited to write the next chapter in my life, always knowing David will be right there beside me.

NOTES

Preface

1. Shute, "The Death of a Loved One: Life's Most Severe Test," pg 10

Chapter One: The Diagnosis

1. The Church of Jesus Christ of Latter-day Saints, *"The Holy Bible"* (New Testament) Luke 22: 42, 1318

2. Crowther, "Life Everlasting," 138

Chapter Two: David's Dream

1. The Church of Jesus Christ of Latter-day Saints, *"The Book of Mormon,"* Mosiah *2:17,* 148-149

Chapter Three: Ups and Downs

1. The Church of Jesus Christ of Latter-day Saints, *"The Doctrine and Covenants," 121: 7-8*, 240

2. The Church of Jesus Christ of Latter-day Saints, *"The Book of Mormon,"* Moroni 7: 45-47, 524

Chapter Four: As I Have Loved You

1. The Church of Jesus Christ of Latter-day Saints, *"The Holy Bible"* (The New Testament) *John 13:34,* 1352

Chapter Five: Trust in the Lord

1. The Church of Jesus Christ of Latter-day Saints, *"The Holy Bible"* (Old Testament) *Proverbs 3:5*, 813

Chapter Six: Mighty Miracles

1. The Church of Jesus Christ of Latter-day Saints, *"The Book of Mormon,"* Alma 26:12, 273

2. Top, "What's On the Other Side," 42

3. The Church of Jesus Christ of Latter-day Saints, *"The Doctrine and Covenants," 84:88*, 159

Chapter Seven: Be Still My Soul

1. The Church of Jesus Christ of Latter-day Saints, *"The Doctrine and Covenants," 6:23*, 12

Chapter Eight: David Our Beloved

1. The Church of Jesus Christ of Latter-day Saints, *"The Holy Bible," (The Old Testament) Psalm 23: 4*, 727

2. The Church of Jesus Christ of Latter-day Saints, *"The Holy Bible," (The New Testament) Acts 10:34*, 1384

Chapter Nine: Angels Among Us

1. The Church of Jesus Christ of Latter-day Saints, *"The Book of Mormon," 2 Nephi 32:3*, 115

2. Crowther, "Life Everlasting," 271

3. Millet, McConkie, "The Life Beyond," 26

4. The Church of Jesus Christ of Latter-day Saints, *"The Doctrine and Covenants," 138:30*, 289

Chapter Ten: David's Life Sketch

1. The Church of Jesus Christ of Latter-day Saints, *"The Book of Mormon," Moroni 7:47*, 524

2. The Church of Jesus Christ of Latter-day Saints; *"Hymns,"* 165-166

Chapter Eleven: "Let Not Your Heart Be Troubled"

1. The Church of Jesus Christ of Latter-day Saints, *"The New Testament," John 14:26-27*, 1353

NOTES

2. The Church of Jesus Christ of Latter-day Saints, *"Hymns,"* 124

3. Millet, McConkie *"The Life Beyond,"* 119

Chapter Twelve: Ministering Angels

1. The Church of Jesus Christ of Latter-day Saints, *"The Doctrine and Covenants,"* 130:5, 264

2. Millet, McConkie, *"The Life Beyond,"* 73

3. Richardson, *"The Message,"* 54

4. Richardson, *"The Message,"* 87

5. Millet, "The Life Beyond," 77

6. The Church of Jesus Christ of Latter-day Saints, *"Teachings of the Presidents of the Church,"* 226

7. Parry, "Angels, Agents of Light, Love, and Power," 130

8. Millet, McConkie, *"The Life Beyond,"* 77

9. Top, "What's On The Other Side," 34

10. Crowther, "Life Everlasting," 260

Chapter Thirteen: Treasured Testimonies

1. The Church of Jesus Christ of Latter-day Saints, *"The Book of Mormon,"* Moroni 10:5, *529*

2. Cory Maxwell, "The Neil A Maxwell Quote Book," 385

WORKS CITED

Crowther, Duane S. *Life Everlasting-a Definitive Study of Life after Death*. Cedar Fort: Horizon Publishers, 2008

Maxwell, Cory. *The Neil A. Maxwell Quote Book*. Salt Lake City, Deseret Book Co, 2009

Millet, Robert L, McConkie, Joseph Fielding. *The Life Beyond*. Salt Lake City: Book craft Inc, 1986

Parry, Donald W. *Angels, Agents of Light, Love, and Power*. Salt Lake: Deseret Book Co, 2013

Richardson, Lance. *The Message*. American Falls: American Family Publications, 2000

Shute, Wayne R. The Death of a Loved One -Life's Most Severe Test. Orem, Millennial Press, 2013

Top, Brent L. *What's On the Other Side?* Salt Lake City: Deseret Book Co, 2012

The Church of Jesus Christ of Latter-day Saints. *Hymns of the Church of Jesus Christ of Latter-day Saints*. Salt Lake City: Deseret Book Co, 1985

The Church of Jesus Christ of Latter-day Saints. *Teachings of the Presidents of the Church*. Salt Lake City: Intellectual Reserve Inc, 2007

The Church of Jesus Christ of Latter-day Saints. The Holy Bible, The Book of Mormon, The Doctrine Covenants, The Pearl of Great Price: Intellectual Reserve Inc, 1979

Made in the USA
Charleston, SC
27 June 2014